Haunted

Tara Flynn

If These Wigs Could Talk

Panti Bliss

methuen | drama

LONDON • NEW YORK • OXFORD • NEW DELHI • SYDNEY

METHUEN DRAMA

Bloomsbury Publishing Plc

50 Bedford Square, London, WC1B 3DP, UK

1385 Broadway, New York, NY 10018, USA

29 Earlsfort Terrace, Dublin 2, Ireland

BLOOMSBURY, METHUEN DRAMA and the Methuen
Drama logo are trademarks of Bloomsbury Publishing Plc

First published in Great Britain 2022

Cover design: Niall Sweeney

Cover photo © Patricio Cassinoni

A catalogue record for this book is available from the British Library.

A catalog record for this book is available from the Library of Congress.

ISBN: PB: 978-1-3503-8314-2
ePDF: 978-1-3503-8315-9
eBook: 978-1-3503-8316-6

Series: Modern Plays

Typeset by Mark Heslington Ltd, Scarborough, North Yorkshire

To find out more about our authors and books visit
www.bloomsbury.com and sign up for our newsletters.

THISISPOPBABY AND THE ABBEY THEATRE PRESENT

HAUNTED

By Tara Flynn

IF THESE WIGS COULD TALK

By Panti Bliss

Haunted by Tara Flynn and *If These Wigs Could Talk* by Panti Bliss premiered on the Peacock Stage at the Abbey Theatre in November 2022, in a co-production from THISISPOPBABY and The Abbey Theatre, supported by The Arts Council, Dublin City Council and The Irish Hospice Foundation.

Creative Team: If These Wigs Could Talk

Written and Performed by	Panti Bliss
Director and Dramaturg	Phillip McMahon
Set Design by	Molly O'Cathain
Costume Design by	James David Seaver
Lighting Design by	Sinéad McKenna
Sound Design by	Jenny O'Malley
Associate Director	Chris Moran
Produced by	Jennifer Jennings and Laura Rigney
Production Manager	Adam Fitzsimons
Stage Manager	Evie McGuinness
Production Associate	Adam Doyle
PR Manager	Conleth Teevan
Graphic Design	Niall Sweeney, Pony Ltd
Publicity Image	Pato Cassinoni
Promotional Video	Olga Kuzmenko

Creative Team: Haunted

Written and Performed by	Tara Flynn
Director and Dramaturg	Phillip McMahon
Set and Costume Design by	Molly O'Cathain
Lighting Design by	Sinéad McKenna
Sound Design by	Jenny O'Malley
Associate Director	Chris Moran
Produced by	Jennifer Jennings and Laura Rigney
Production Manager	Adam Fitzsimons
Stage Manager	Olivia Drennan
Production Associate	Adam Doyle
PR Manager	Conleth Teevan
Graphic Design	Niall Sweeney, Pony Ltd
Publicity Image	Pato Cassinoni
Promotional Video	Olga Kuzmenko

THISISPOPBABY AND THE ABBEY THEATRE PRESENT

HAUNTED

By Tara Flynn

IF THESE WIGS COULD TALK

By Panti Bliss

Haunted by Tara Flynn and *If These Wigs Could Talk* by Panti Bliss premiered on the Peacock Stage at the Abbey Theatre in November 2022, in a co-production from THISISPOPBABY and The Abbey Theatre, supported by The Arts Council, Dublin City Council and The Irish Hospice Foundation.

Creative Team: If These Wigs Could Talk

Written and Performed by	Panti Bliss
Director and Dramaturg	Phillip McMahon
Set Design by	Molly O'Cathain
Costume Design by	James David Seaver
Lighting Design by	Sinéad McKenna
Sound Design by	Jenny O'Malley
Associate Director	Chris Moran
Produced by	Jennifer Jennings and Laura Rigney
Production Manager	Adam Fitzsimons
Stage Manager	Evie McGuinness
Production Associate	Adam Doyle
PR Manager	Conleth Teevan
Graphic Design	Niall Sweeney, Pony Ltd
Publicity Image	Pato Cassinoni
Promotional Video	Olga Kuzmenko

Creative Team: Haunted

Written and Performed by	Tara Flynn
Director and Dramaturg	Phillip McMahon
Set and Costume Design by	Molly O'Cathain
Lighting Design by	Sinéad McKenna
Sound Design by	Jenny O'Malley
Associate Director	Chris Moran
Produced by	Jennifer Jennings and Laura Rigney
Production Manager	Adam Fitzsimons
Stage Manager	Olivia Drennan
Production Associate	Adam Doyle
PR Manager	Conleth Teevan
Graphic Design	Niall Sweeney, Pony Ltd
Publicity Image	Pato Cassinoni
Promotional Video	Olga Kuzmenko

The Abbey Theatre

As Ireland's national theatre, the Abbey Theatre's ambition is to enrich the cultural lives of everyone with a curiosity for and interest in Irish theatre, stories, artists and culture. Courage and imagination is at the heart of our storytelling, while inclusivity, diversity and equality are at the core of our thinking. Our art celebrates both the rich canon of Irish dramatic writing and the potential of future generations of Irish theatre artists.

Ireland has a rich history of theatre and playwriting and extraordinary actors, designers and directors.

Our artists are at the heart of this organisation, with Marina Carr and Conor McPherson as Senior Associate Playwrights and Caroline Byrne as Associate Director. The Abbey is delighted to be working with four Resident Directors – Gea Gojak, Claire O'Reilly, Laura Sheeran and Colm Summers.

As we find and champion new voices and new ways of seeing, we are identifying combinations of characters we are yet to meet on our stages, having conversations we are yet to hear. We are also engaging in an interrogation of our classical canon with an urgency about what makes it speak to this moment. Our stories teach us what it is to belong, and what it is to be excluded and exclude. Artistically our programme is built on these twin impulses, and around two questions: 'who were we, and who are we now?'

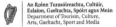

Principal Partner:

BANK OF AMERICA

An Roinn Turasóireachta, Cultúir,
Ealaíon, Gaeltachta, Spóirt agus Meán
Department of Tourism, Culture,
Arts, Gaeltacht, Sport and Media

Tara Flynn

Tara works extensively as an actor, writer and voice artist in theatre, radio and TV. Her previous one-woman show *Not a Funny Word* (THISISPOPBABY in association with the Abbey Theatre) played to sold-out crowds. *Haunted* will be presented by THISISPOPBABY at the Peacock in late 2022.

A popular MC, she was a core member of Dublin Comedy Improv for many years. TV acting work includes *Moone Boy*, *Stewart Lee's Comedy Vehicle* and *Line of Duty*. She's written three books: *Rage-In*, *You're Grand* and *Giving Out Yards*.

She's been a vocal campaigner for reproductive rights and the repeal of Ireland's Eighth Amendment. She currently co-hosts comedy problem-solving podcast *Now You're Asking with Marian Keyes and Tara Flynn* for BBC Radio 4 and BBC Sounds.

Tara lives in Dublin with her husband Carl.

Panti

Panti Bliss is a writer, performer, pub landlady, 'gender discombobulist' and 'accidental activist', and has been a fixture of Ireland's gay community since the late 80s.

She played a central role in the campaign for marriage equality in Ireland and, in 2014, a speech she made in the Abbey Theatre about oppression and what it is to be LGBTI+ in Ireland became an international sensation. It was lauded as one of the world's great speeches, put to music by Pet Shop Boys, and turned her into an iconic figure for equality in Ireland.

Panti has written and performed five one-woman shows which have toured extensively across Ireland, the UK, Europe, the US and Australia, and was in the cast of the acclaimed show *RIOT*. Her memoir *Woman in the Making* was published in 2014, and she was the subject of a major documentary in 2015 called *The Queen of Ireland*. Her plaudits include a Person of the Year Award and an honorary doctorate from Trinity College Dublin.

Panti continues to tour internationally with her live shows, has presented an award-winning radio show – *Pantisocracy* – on RTE for a number of years, is much in demand as a public speaker, and has travelled extensively on behalf of the Irish Department of Foreign Affairs and Irish Aid.

She also owns a pub.

When not touring, Panti lives in Dublin with a dog, a cat, and the current Mr Bliss.

Phillip McMahon

Phillip McMahon is a playwright and director based in Dublin.

Writing credits include *Once Before I Go, Come on Home, Town Is Dead, Alice in Funderland, Pineapple, Elevator, Investment Potential, All Over Town* and *Danny and Chantelle (still here)*.

Directing credits include *Straight to Video* and *Dublin Oldschool* by Emmet Kirwan, *Town Is Dead* for The Abbey Theatre, *Insane Animals* by Bourgeois & Maurice, *Not A Funny Word* by Tara Flynn and *Money* by Peter Daly. He has made and toured a number of smash hit shows with long-time collaborator, drag superstar Panti, and was co-producer and co-writer on Conor Horgan's esteemed documentary *The Queen of Ireland* for Blinder Films. Philip recently co-created a dance theatre work, *Party Scene,* with long-time collaborator, choreographer Philip Connaughton.

Phillip is co-founder and co-director of theatre production company THISISPOPBABY, wherein he was co-creator and co-curator of the THISISPOPBABY performance venue at Electric Picnic Music and Arts Festival, Queer Notions cross arts festival, WERK Performance/Art/Club and Where We Live festival of performance and ideas. Phillip has created and directed many works within THISISPOPBABY, including international hit *RIOT* and, more recently, *WAKE*, at Dublin's National Stadium.

Phillip was a former Writer in Association at the Abbey Theatre, Dublin. He is currently Artistic Associate at the Lyric Hammersmith Theatre, London, and is Research Fellow at the Birkbeck Centre for Contemporary Theatre, London.

Molly O'Cathain

Molly O'Cathain is a Set and Costume Designer based in Dublin working across theatre, dance, opera and various other art forms. She is a founding member and Company Designer for award-winning Malaprop Theatre.

Previous designs for THISISPOPBABY include *Shit* (Costume Design/ Project Arts Centre).

Molly's recent credits include *Bajazet* (Irish National Opera / Royal Opera House/ Best Opera Production Olivier Award nomination); *An Octoroon* (Costume Design/Abbey Theatre); *Absent The Wrong* (Set Design/Abbey Theatre); *Constellations* (Gate Theatre); *It Was Easy (in the end)* (Abbey /THEATREclub); *Ask Too Much of Me* (Abbey/ NYT); *Minseach* (Sibeal Davitt Dance); *The Playboy of The Western World* (Dublin Theatre Festival/The Gaiety Theatre/The Lyric Belfast); and *To the Lighthouse* (The Everyman/Hatch Productions). Her designs for Malaprop Theatre include: *Where Sat the Lovers, Before You Say Anything, Everything Not Saved, BlackCatfishMusketeer* and *LOVE+*.

James McGlynn Seaver

James McGlynn Seaver is an Irish Costume Designer and Costume maker. Over the last twelve years Seaver has been collaborating and creating the enviable wardrobe of Ireland's 'National Treasure', Panti Bliss, whose dress worn at the now famous 'Noble Call' speech at the Abbey Theatre in 2014 currently resides in the National Museum at Collins Barracks. With a passion for the evolution of fashion through the ages, Seaver reproduces and reconceptualises historic garments for film and private clients as well as being a bespoke corset maker. Seaver currently serves as the head of costume at the Gate Theatre in Dublin.

Sinéad McKenna

Sinéad McKenna is an internationally-renowned designer working across theatre, opera, dance and film. She has won two Irish Times Theatre Awards for Best Lighting Design and a Drama Desk nomination for Best Lighting Design for a Musical.

Previous designs for THISISPOPBABY include *Alice in Funderland* and *Elevator.*

Other recent designs include *HEAVEN* (Fishamble/NYC); *Walking with Ghosts, Straight to Video* and *The Approach* (Landmark Productions/ NYC); *The Tales of Hoffmann, Maria Stuarda, Griselda, La Bohéme* (Irish National Opera); *Faith Healer, Drama at Inish, The Unmanageable Sisters, Othello, Aristocrats* and *The Plough and the Stars* (Abbey Theatre); *Dēmos* (Liz Roche Company), *Parade* (Théâtre du Châtelet, Paris) and *Angela's Ashes: The Musical* (Bord Gais/Tour).

Chris Moran

Chris Moran is a theatre director and writer from Co. Wicklow. Recent work includes *The Importance of Being Earnest* (Stagedoor Manor, USA); *A Normal Woman* (TalentLAB programme, Théâtres de la ville de Luxembourg); *The Song Collector* (Galway Theatre Festival) and *Homos, or Everyone in America* (The Lir). He was Associate Director for ANU Productions' *Faultline* (Gate Theatre co-production, Dublin Theatre Festival). He also creates theatre for and with young people in Ireland and Europe. Chris trained at the Lir, the National Academy of Dramatic Art. He is a TRANSFORM Associate Artist at the Mermaid Arts Centre, Bray, 2022–3.

Jenny O'Malley

Jenny is a composer and sound designer based in Dublin who is a classically trained multi-instrumentalist and vocalist. Some of her theatre credits include *Summertime* (Dublin Fringe Festival 2018/ Drogheda Arts Festival 2019/Abbey Young Curators Festival 2019); *Iphigenia in Splott* (Smock Alley Theatre 2018); *We Can't Have Monkeys in The House* (Peacock Theatre 2019); *Sauce* (Bewley's Cafe Theatre 2019 and 2022); *Restoration* (Project Arts Centre 2020); *Venus in Fur* (Project Arts Centre 2020); *SHIT* (Project Arts Centre 2020 and 2022); *Will I See You There* (Dublin Fringe Festival 2020); *Before You Say Anything* (Dublin Fringe Festival 2020); *Ar Ais Arís* (Brightening Air 2021/Galway Arts Festival 2021/Cairde Arts Festival 2022/Earagail Arts Festival 2022); *Goodnight Egg* (Civic Theatre 2021); *Where Sat the Lovers* (Dublin Fringe Festival 2021); *Masterclass* (Dublin Fringe Festival 2021/True Northern Arts Festival Harstad 2022/Edinburgh Fringe Festival 2022); *You're Still Here* (Dublin Fringe Festival 2021); *The Libravian* (Baboró Arts Festival 2021/Ottawa Children's Festival 2022/Cairde Arts Festival 2022); *Absent The Wrong* (Dublin Fringe Festival 2022) and *Good Sex* (Dublin Theatre Festival 2022).

Jennifer Jennings

Jennifer Jennings is a theatre and festival maker based in Dublin. She is co-founder and co-director of acclaimed Irish theatre company THISISPOPBABY, Arts Director of Beyond the Pale Music Festival and Artistic Director in Residence at UCD's Creative Futures Academy.

For THISISPOPBABY, highlights include co-directing the recent smash hit *WAKE* (Judges' Special Award Dublin Fringe 2022), and the international sensation *RIOT* (Best Production, Dublin Fringe 2016); directing *Shit* by Patricia Cornelius and family show *Absolute Legends* for Lords of Strut; curating Where We Live Festivals 2018 and 2020, Queer Notions Arts Festival 2009 and 2010, *POPTENT* at Electric Picnic 2008–2010 and WERK performance art club (The Abbey Theatre, IMMA and Melbourne Festival); and producing Panti's *High Heels in Low Places* (World Tour 2015–17 / Soho Live films 2018), *Sure Look It, Fuck It* by Clare Dunne and *Alice in Funderland – A New Musical* by Phillip McMahon and Raymond Scannell.

Previously, Jennifer has been Artistic Director of Neon Lights Music and Arts Festival (Singapore), Arts Programme Director of Harvest Music Festival (Sydney, Melbourne, Brisbane), Head of Programming at Abbotsford Convent Melbourne and Programme Director for Dublin Fringe Festival.

Laura Rigney

Laura Rigney is an Irish Arts Manager and Cultural Producer. She is General Manager with THISISPOPBABY and Co-Producer of *Haunted* by Tara Flynn and *If These Wigs Could Talk* by Panti Bliss.

She has worked extensively in the arts and non-profit creative organisations leading, developing and providing consultancy in areas of creative and business development, arts management, festivals and event management.

Previously, Laura was Director of Design Galway, Fundraiser with Galway International Arts Festival, Development and Partnership Manager with Galway 2020 – European Capital of Culture, Marketing and Development Manager with Macnas – Spectacle and Street Performance Company. She has worked as a consultant in areas of strategic and creative development for Baboró International Arts Festival for Children, Tulca Festival of Visual Arts and Traditional Irish Music Festival, Fleadh Cheoil na hÉireann.

A big THISISPOPBABY thank you to our incredible Pop Heroes

Daire Hickey, James Morris, Oisín Clarke, Maeve Houlihan, Anthony Boushel, Billy McGrath, Dennis Jennings, Louise O'Reilly, Mick Connell, Martin Spillane, Collette Farrell, Lara Hickey, Ultan Dillon, Donal Beecher, Ailbhe Smyth, Ciara Cuffe, Christine Delany, Collette Farrell, David Tighe, Emer McLysaght, Emily Mark, Helena Murphy, John King, Miriam Haughton, Nicola Rogers, Noel Minogue, Suzy Byrne, Seamus Cahill.

Haunted

Tara   The best thing about hitting the floor, is that everything stops.

Feels like there's nowhere left to fall. *Thunk*! Floor.
You've lost everything. Your marbles, everything.
You don't even have falling to fear anymore – that's all behind you now. And what better place to look for your marbles than the floor!

'Away with the fairies'. That's what they call it, when you're 'Not quite in your head.' When you're 'Having a bit of a break.' Slipped off to a darker world, that looks like ours, but isn't.

Woooooh . . .

My therapist says I use humour to deflect. [*Silly voice.*] Silly voices, so it's not quite me. That I flip serious things, that are actually not funny at all. But he's wrong. THEY'RE TOTALLY FECKING HILARIOUS.

It's nice. Here on the floor.

I'm thinking about one beautiful day, not too long ago. Sitting in my therapist's office in a gorgeous suburb of Dublin, by the sea. Leafy. Y'know, yachts. I've a giant coffee in my lap – the unethical kind that'd put a small café out of business – but I need it: I haven't slept. For months. So I gulp down the corporate guilt along with the caffeine.

And I'm shaking. I'm shaking and shaking – the giant coffee's about to spill and cause localised flooding – but the therapist is saying 'Don't you feel great? It must be amazing!'

You see, [*Shakes.*] what you're looking at, right here, is a winner.

In the last three years, I've been called everything from 'hero' to 'witch', by people I've never even met.
Because I told a secret.
Abortion. I'd had one. People needed them, always will.
Ireland's constitution said 'no'.

This therapist has let me come see him – for free – his gift to some of us who campaigned to repeal Ireland's Eighth Amendment.
We didn't have offices, we weren't in fancy-dan political parties or anything, but we worked our butts off – for free – on the referendum campaign to change the constitution.

Which is why, on the day of the Yes result, the lovely therapist says 'You must feel great?!'

He seems to think this is the end of the story. Can't he feel me shaking? I'm sure it must be causing tremors in the sea.

Something dawns on him. Something we've only touched on before. Something we glossed over as we dealt with abuse in the moment, putting out campaign-related fires. *BAM. KAPOW.*
'Of course, now,' he says 'you're free to deal with the grief.'

See, just months before I shared my secret with the world, my dad died.

In the three years since, there hasn't been time for grief. As soon as the secret was out, the campaign whirlwind pitched me high into the air, whipped me mercilessly around – think 1996 film *Twister*. Pulling in cars. Horses. Trees.
I won't see the ground again for ages, not till three years later, when I hit the floor. *Thunk.*

For a second, the shaking coffee stops. And then it starts straight up again.

The sky comes off. That's what happens when a parent dies. It might be a stormy sky, or a sunny one. It's complicated. But it's your sky. And now it's gone.

Now we're here, me and my marbles, all over the floor.

Tara   Away with the fairies.

They say that long ago, the gaps between worlds were narrower. Fairies could – *slip!* – between them.

Some women were in touch with that other world. Healers. Witches. Banshees. Like Biddy Early, the wise woman who lived in the 1800s, in my dad's village in County Clare.

I don't believe in ghosts. I mean, I believe in ghost *stories* – I've got Discovery +. Ghosts have never been a hotter ticket. Them and True Crime. I'd nearly kidnap myself if I thought I'd get a telly gig out of it.
I don't believe in ghosts. But I do have a scary story.

My dad shot Santa Claus.

You have to understand, they were *different times!* Like racists say about *then* when they want to say racist stuff *now*. *Different times!*

Christmas Eve, Ireland, 1978. I'm nine years old, probably wearing corduroy trousers. Cool. Cords. We're in the family car, driving home from a friend's Kris Kringle party. Twinkly lights, German chocolate. Oh, fierce glam: in County Cork, until a month ago, we only had one television channel. Some American detective shows: lots of smoking and running (in cords), amazing sideburns, but mostly homegrown stuff: cattle marts, hurling matches and Mass for a treat on Sundays.

Really. *Mart and Market* was a massive hit. Cows walking around in a circle, for sale. Ads for aftershave and tractor safety.

One huge show was called *In My Father's Time*. A *seanchaí* – an old Irish storyteller – on telly. From an old-timey kitchen, he'd . . .
[**Seanchaí** *voice.*] *tell tales from the past, familiar stories retold.*
Tara   Don't ask me why the famous seanchaís are all from Kerry. Being from Cork, I take it personally.
Seanchaí   *These stories were to make everyone feel good about themselves, d'you see? How different now, in the with-it 70s, from backwards-then, with their cattle marts, hurling matches and Mass for a treat on Sundays.*

Tara   Change in Ireland. It's slow.
Seanchaís were the ones who got to tell your story. You better hope they liked you.

Anyway, 1978 German Christmas Eve was cool. And myself and my sister are on a chocolate hiiiigh!
But there's a problem: we just got small presents from 'Kris'. Did that mean that now the Real Santa was gonna fly our 'real' presents straight over our house in disgust?
Ho ho NO.

Full disclosure: I don't believe in Santa. I'm nine. I've lived. You can probably tell from my cords.

Oh. You should probably also know that I'm possessed.

Yeah! No one was more surprised than me. Dad told me. You can't say the man didn't love drama. He'd wanted to be an actor, but that didn't work out: no one was an actor in his day, no one from Clare. He wanted to be posh, but sure look . . . He was strict. 'On time means two minutes early. Leave time for two punctures.' To this day, if I'm one minute late, I break into a sweat, even on the bus, where I'm not even the one in charge of the punctures.
Being LATE meant WRATH. Six foot two, booming-voiced wrath. You did not want the wrath. You never knew what would trigger the wrath. And not being able to keep my big mouth shut, I was a wrath magnet.

About a year earlier, I'd tried to stand up to him. To make my small self big. I roared, or slammed a door, and he announced I was possessed: I should be taken to a priest. Priests were still big in Ireland in the 70s. Them and cords. Of course, demonic possession was huge then too: if there wasn't a spinning head jump-scare, had you even been to the cinema?
And of course I knew about demons. I went to a Catholic school.
My dad had a troubled relationship with the Church. On-again, off-again, kinda thing. But he wouldn't be beyond throwing a bit of old Catholicism into the wrath, for spice.

Now, was I an annoying little weirdo? Yes! My hair was wild
– not straight and shiny like Dad's. 'Banshee!' he'd say.
Combing just made it worse.
I had an extremely deep voice for my age. At eight, I could
sing all the low notes in Carpenters' songs.
'After long enough of being alone . . .'
Oh it's fine now, but at eight? Alert the Pope.
I loved to sing in the car. Dad hated it: 'Shut up, you crow.'
But different times! He was just practising Excellent 70s
Parenting, crushing notions out of me and and me back into
place.

My little sister was good at avoiding the wrath. I was more of
what you'd call a fool. Deflecting the wrath away from her.
Not cos I'm good or anything, I just couldn't keep my trap
shut.
Cos his temper, his fire was in me, too. That scared me. I
promised myself: I will not be like him.

Anyway, car, Christmas Eve, I'm keeping the Santa charade
going for my sis. What harm? I too like getting stuff. There's
a Carpenters album in it for me: *The Singles: 1974–1978*.
But the stress: will the Real Santa come, or won't he? Our
little voices rising in pitch.
Even mine.
Things are getting heated. Then they go stone cold.

'Santa Claus is dead. I shot him.'

My father grips the wheel and navigates the frosty road
ahead. A dark and lonely road. You wouldn't know it if you
didn't know. He's smoking: more Excellent 70s Parenting:

• after several glasses of Gluhwein, you'd need a cigarette
  to sober you up for the drive.

• Everyone smoked in the car. How else could you
  acclimatise kids to the blue haze they'd encounter in
  later life, in pubs or doctors' offices?

'Santa's dead. I shot him.' He exhales and accelerates, like in one of those detective shows.

My mother shrieks in the passenger seat. My sister starts to cry.

Santa's not real. He didn't shoot Santa, as far as we can be sure – True Crime hadn't been invented yet. But what hung in the car like smoke was the saying of it. The cruelty, the aim to shock and hurt. That's what we breathed in.

Santa did come, in the end. Even after his traumatic evening. The Carpenters album landed safe and sound. And Dad was in good form too. As if the night before hadn't happened. *Merry Christmas!* Life's easier, sometimes, if you just shut up and smile.

[*Floor.*]
Tara   Away with the fairies, you can't think, but you're thinking all the time.

The first time that my father cheated death, he was twenty-two. He fell off a horse and into a coma, for twelve whole days. Everyone thought he would die. There wasn't a lot to do in his village – they didn't even have electricity yet – so stories were very important. People love other people's misery. Loads of the tales were of Biddy Early, who'd lived only a small way out the road.

Seanchaí   *Biddy talked to fairies. She could see the future in her magic bottle. She could cure you, but she mightn't!*
Whether she was good or bad . . . depends who's telling the story.

Tara   So when Dad was at death's door, the gossip around the village! The suspense! He was almost certain to die.

AND THEN HE DIDN'T FECKING DIE.

For a Clareman my father was, as we say in Cork, 'haunted'. 'Haunted' means so lucky it'd make ya sick. You must have a good ghost, helping you.

He was owed some luck: his mother died of breast cancer when he was sixteen. Now, with young sisters to provide for . . . no being an actor. No being posh. He grieved his mother his whole life. So unfair. Too early for early detection. Too late for Biddy Early.

Seanchaí   *Away with the fairies.*

Tara   Like me, Seanchaí! Away with the fairies, on the floor, not a marble in sight.

Seanchaí   *Fairies were powerful. Frightening. They could change shape, to look like you, or me, but never fully settle in our world Fairies, now, loved mischief: they spent their days leading cows astray or stealing the odd child, leaving a changeling in its place. The real child left to wander below in their world.*

Tara   Before I shared my secret, I was a bit of a tool. In my forties, married, living in Dublin, acting and writing; the possession clearly hadn't done me any harm.

[*Spotlight.*]
Fame didn't interest me. Not really. I was happy being just well-known enough to get more work. Fame-adjacent, maybe.
I wrote funny magazine columns; people's coffee mugs leaving a ring around my head on the page. I used my unusual voice to play Molly the Morbeg, a huge hit with the under-fives, and the Caramel Bunny – *Hey there, Mr. Squirrel* – a huge hit with the under-fifties. (Who knew chocolate boners were a thing?) But I only played her once and only in Ireland. Which kind of sums up my career.
I've never been in *VIP*: Ireland's foremost celeb magazine.
NTIAP: Not That Important A Person.
I don't get sent free stuff. Unbox? Me? Never. I've been at maybe two glittering awards ceremonies.
Like, you'd know me, but *from where?*
Fame-adjacent.

I was once the Face of Poo. Me and my dog photographed by the Council, to promote picking up shite. Hardly a Chanel endorsement, but look, I was around and Keira Knightley is a very busy woman.

My work didn't make a huge difference, except maybe to the soles of your shoes. You're welcome. If I made people feel a bit better, or gave them the odd chocolate boner, life was good.

But in 2015, it was time to share the secret. To stop shutting up and smiling. I didn't want to. But something drove me. Told me it was now.

From that moment, the damn spotlight never went off.

[*Spotlight goes off.*]

Tara   In case you're not up to speed on world events, mouthy women don't exactly get a warm reception. Here in Ireland, we raised it to an art form, locking up women in laundries if they were too sassy, or brazen, or their lipstick was too bright. We did this until 1996. No wonder we were over it.

Now, no one I know ever went: 'D'you know what I think I'll be? An activist!' They just cared enough to put the rest of their lives on hold, to try effect some change.

In the run up to the referendum, we knocked on doors. Wore badges. Gave talks. Volunteered whatever skills we had.

And some of us shared the most private bit of ourselves. Our wombs – *hello!* Tragic stories and everyday ones, like mine. Because – guess what, world? An outright ban didn't stop people getting abortions. Of course not. Just made them unsafe. But they knew that.

Now, Irish women had written their stories before. Spoken them in our Parliament. Tweeted them. Relentless campaigners – real heroes – at it for decades when they seemed like outliers, alone. Whatever scrap of courage I had came from them. And this time, the wind was behind us.

Political lads had a field day:
(*In a condescending tone.*) 'Back in yeer boxes now, ladies. Ye're doing it wrong! You're putting people off with yeer screeching.'

But we took our story back. 'Grassroots,' they call campaigns like that. Ground up.
Ground . . . Like the lovely floor.

Ireland voted. And we won. The pushback was pretty immediate, but we did win.
But the commentary. The comments.
I'm used to reviews of my work: 'Not funny, big-nose!' Now what everyone is analysing, dissecting, is me.
Having a platform – even one built on chocolate boners – is a privilege. People listen when you speak. But parasocial relationships are dangerous. They think they know you, but they don't really, so they fill in blanks with assumptions and made up shit. *Your fave is problematic* – on a pedestal one day, gleefully kicked off it the next. So, praise makes me nervous. Call myself a hero, are you mad?
But that's not what people are saying, now we've won.

So many of us had a similar story. The difference between mine and others who told theirs . . .?
Mine was one of those 'bad' abortions, one I chose. And then, thicko that I am, I never went on to redeem myself by becoming a mother. Heartless and cold, it was easy to make a monster out of me. Fun, too, it seems. Plus: my part all. Played out. In public.

———————————

Seanchaí   *Who. The fuck. Does she think. She is?*

In the year 2015, the English band Blur were on a bit of a comeback, headlining Electric Picnic – a kind of a festival that's not so much picnics, more kebabs. And there, on a stage in a tent, didn't herself tell about travelling for an abortion.

Now, was that a bit risky and she in the show-biz? Was she jeopardising any potential spon-con collabs with this controversy? Yes! And herself was sick with nerves. But up she got, and the words scorched out of her.

Tara   There wasn't a huge crowd at that Amnesty International event that day, but the tent is almost full: *She Is Not A Criminal*, it's called. Putting a face to 'people who travel for healthcare'. Me. Even if you're not quite sure where you know this face from.

My husband's in the front row, ready to fight.

– He grew up a black kid in Los Angeles in the 80s; I grew up in Kinsale, where the local ghost is literally called the White Lady. Our backgrounds are so different –

He's tense: in America, abortion gets people edgy. Even worse than Ireland, where we just didn't talk about it at all.

In that crowd are journalists. An anti-choice person at the back tries a bit of scaremongering, but she soon pulls back. It turns out she's the outlier; other people share their stories, too, right there in that tent. We're not alone. We all know someone. We're everywhere.

The event wraps up, less fraught than we all expected.

We drive away from the festival: me, the husband and the dog. (I only let the dog drive part of the way.) We're not sure what will have changed, but maybe . . . Maybe nothing? Because scary as it was, that went well.

We check into a fancy hotel – our holiday for the year – and blend. Posh guests hide behind sunglasses and you *know* I do too. I'm one of the freaking *Real Housewives*.

[*Housewife tagline.*]

'You can take the girl out of Cork, but I'll never put a cork . . . in it.'

But I don't throw drinks in anyone's face. Don't want the attention. Because maybe things are still the same.

Breakfast the next day. Fancy dining room. Silver coffee pots and the good veggie sausages; they never have those. Free Sunday papers. Leafing, idly leafing while the piano tinkles

away. And – bam – there I am. On the page. My most
personal bits. Covered in other people's toast crumbs.
One headline: 'Comedian talked about her abortion at
Electric Picnic . . .' Like I had it there. If we'd been able to
get them at festivals, we wouldn't have been in the mess we
were in.
I'm used to seeing my name in print. This time I hadn't
written the words. This time, it wasn't funny.

It feels like everyone's eggs benedicts freeze halfway to their
mouths. They turn, like in *The Exorcist*, and stare, from
behind their oversized Tom Fords.
I spend most of the rest of the trip hiding out in the room.
Because, from now on . . . everyone has . . . an opinion!

Commenters   *She had sex, the hussy. I hear she has a giant
vagina.*
She doesn't regret a thing! Giant vagina!
She wants all abortions, all the time. Giant giant vagina!

Tara   Social media. Flagship radio shows. Politicians
pontificate. I'm public property now – I'm NEWS – and
everyone decides they have a right of way.
And my phone goes *ping*.
Ping.
Ping. Ping. Ping.

[*Game show music plays.*]
Tara (*in the style of a gameshow host*)   *Let's play: STFU! The show
where we know that all the opinions all the time is completely
counterproductive. Oh they're fun to have, but nothing –
ABSOLUTELY NOTHING – gets solved. We ask 'Is my input
required?' At STFU we say, sometimes, we all really should just
SHUT THE FUCK UP.*
Do I have personal experience of the issue? No? Then [*Encouraging
the audience to join in.*] *SHUT THE FUCK UP!*
Have I studied it at length? No? Then SHUT THE FUCK UP!
Have people with personal experience or who've studied it at length

already had their say? Yes? Then SHUT THE FUCK UP?
And now, time for our favourite category:

Is this JUST YOUR FUCKING OPINION? If so, then,
GERTRUDE, SWEETIE, HAVE YOU CONSIDERED
SHUTTING THE FUCKING FUCK UP.

Tara   Opinions are great. But they lose power when we're
all just having them all the time.

Tara   Highlights from the centre of a whirlwind:

- I'm discussed in local papers. Interviewed by Canadian
  TV, German broadsheets, Spanish blogs. I get emotional
  sometimes. Beg them not to use any teary footage.
  'Please, they'll say I'm fake.' They do.

- My image is photoshopped, pithy t-shirts about murder.
  But look, I've never had merch before, not even for the
  poo thing.

- A political party member tweets that I – quote – 'wasn't
  bothered' to be pregnant, 'why is she a feminist icon?'

His party apologises on the radio. I don't hear it, but my
mother does. She's been so worried.

[*Ping.*]
Commenters   *This is what it's like to be a woman in the public*
eye! She asked for this!
I don't know what her reasons for going public were, but they were
wrong!
Why don't you just switch your phone off?

Tara   Like I haven't thought of that, Sheila. I do turn it off.
But they're all still at it when I switch back on.
Each PING a little piercing of my skin.

There is support. A lot of it behind closed doors.
'You're so brave, but you understand that publicly I have to
say *durty durty giant vagina*?'

A constant spotlight can sear you, like a laser, till it cuts through to bone.

Tara   But maybe this is what I was born to do? I've been a lightning rod in the campaign – a rodeo clown, drawing danger away from others, providing comic relief. Maybe taking wrath is what I'm for?

The second time my father cheated death, I was in my teens. The giant just started wilting before our eyes. They don't know why.
Hospital. Too sick for us to see him. It's painful in the house, but peaceful, too. It's complicated. He fades and fades. We wait. Months and a thousand tests later, they say it's a kind of leukemia that's not really leukemia, it's benign. Coulda fooled us. It's not nothing. He's fading, fading, fading . . .

AND THEN HE DIDN'T FECKING DIE.

They take out his spleen and he rallies. Comes home. He's upbeat and affectionate. *Who's this guy?* Full of the joys of gratitude and spring. But it doesn't last. Soon, he's back to his icy, fiery self.

He could have had a better family, you know.

What I'm saying is, I'm used to wrath. I'd been braced for shite from anti-choice extremists. They have a certain style. What I hadn't expected was the friendly fire. That sometimes our own official campaign doors shut on those of us who came to be called *The Women Who Told Their Stories*. Especially durty ones like me. Kept to the back, until it was time to *win hearts and minds,* when we'd once again be . . . guided . . . out front.
I hadn't expected that.

Tara   On the day of the referendum results, after therapy, I go to the count centre, to see the votes come in.

Relief.

The lady from Sky News gives me her ear-piece for a live interview back to London.

'Wow. Thank? You?' (Guess we're wax sisters now.)

A kind man gives me his ticket to the official celebrations in Dublin Castle. *I shall go to the ball.* See, although everyone thinks I'm going – *see you there!* – I haven't been invited.

But later that day I find myself standing on the Castle stage. The crowd going wild. I join in:

Yayyyy . . . [*Shaking.*]

The politicians are all delighted with themselves for leaping onto the bandwagon, just in time. Photo ops and backslapping that'd take the wind out of you.
The eyes of the world on us.

[*English.*] *Backwards Ireland backwards no more!*
[*American.*] *Finally free of the shackles of the Catholic Church.*
[*German.*] *Hardly anyone smokes in the car!*

We won.

And I shouldn't be here.

I'm not the only one who wasn't invited. *No one Who Told Their Stories* has.

I mean . . .

On the one hand why should grubby Cinderellas be asked to the fancy castle? This annoying little weirdo did sometimes lose her cool.

Political commentators   *'Ooh, shrill.'*
'Not doing her side any favours.'
'I was going to vote for women's autonomy until she told that troll to fuck off.'

Tara   Nah, ya weren't.

They could never have invited everyone to the Castle stage – thousands worked on this. We'd never all fit. Besides, when *The Women Who Told Our Stories* told our stories, we weren't looking for a cookie.

But Jesus, MAYBE A FECKING CRUMB???
As official accounts get set down, *The Women Who Told Their Stories* are reduced to a couple of lines; afterthoughts, strategies, props. We're often not asked about it at all.

But I got a golden ticket and I'm here. A friend who worked on the campaign drags me up on stage.
'You need to experience the win,' he says, 'or you'll wonder if any of it happened at all.'
He holds my arm aloft
– Yaaaaay –
[*Smiles.*] *I'm fucked. They'll say I'm taking credit. A clout chasing bitch. Who do I think I am? Yaaay! I'm so fucked. Yaaaay.*

Tara   The shaking started the night before. The polls said LANDSLIDE! YES. I couldn't celebrate. I was at a pub, kept needing to lie down. So embarrassing.
There was only one place we wanted to be. To visit Savita – a memorial to her, a mural in town.
Savita Halappanavar died in 2012, denied the abortion she needed because 'This is a Catholic country'. She's the reason so many of us stopped shutting up and smiling. Before her, I'd marched for Choice, MCed fundraisers, as much as I could without really rocking the boat. After Savita, silence wasn't an option.
We asked the bar for candles; they took stubs out of holders. We hopped a cab. And when we reached Savita's beautiful, smiling face, it all just felt too late. The polls say the country was with us: 66.4 per cent. Based on a woman's right to choose. They were even with durty ones like me. And they'd been with us for years.
'I'm sorry,' I said to her picture. 'I'm sorry. I'm sorry. I'm sorry.'
And my body and I began to separate. Gulping, shuddering sobs. Years of poison. Demons. Part of me slithered down drains to somewhere dark and distant. Like an old candle; feeble wisps of smoke are all that's left.

Tara   On the Castle stage next day, politicians smile.
Congratulations! Less than three years on, they'll hand our
new maternity hospital to nuns. We should have known,
their trouser legs still shiny from the kneeling. Glad we were
useful for the photo ops.

I wonder what my dad would think. There's a version where
he's proud. He'd have loved the Castle part. The stage!
In another version, he'd be the first one calling me a witch.
Pointing out how mad my hair is in the pictures.

The big, giant campaign machine is shuddering to a halt.
The Women Who Told Their Stories turn back into pumpkins,
use outlived.

I spot my husband at the front of the crowd. As echoes of
backslapping fade in the courtyard, I climb across the
barricades to him. He holds me up.

Commenters   *You're lucky, y'know? Strong. Things don't affect
you. You bounce.*

Tara   We don't like to think about people not being OK.
Much easier to build a myth.

Seanchaí   *In her heyday, hundreds lined the road to Biddy Early's
house for cures. You bet they'd have got selfies, if they'd phones. She
was the original influencer, all through word of mouth. The Great
Daniel O'Connell went to see could her magic bottle show the results
of a future vote. Didn't he achieve Catholic emancipation! But then
things got bad for Biddy: newly jumped-up priests threatened
excommunication if you went to her. But people went, because
doctors were expensive and Biddy helped for free. She wouldn't say
no to a drop of whiskey though, if you left it at her door.
The people need her, trust her, but they leave ashamed. They whisper
her name, only.*

Tara   A week after all that winning, I'm frightened, though I couldn't tell you, if you asked, what I'm frightened of. Of everything.

Just won't go out. It's nice here on the floor.

Pings.

Commenter   *The way they're glorying in this win is unbecoming.*

Tara   Here I am. Glorying. On the floor. I should never have gone on the stage.
My phone gives me electric shocks. Twitter is making me sick. Opinions still coming thick and fast from people I don't know.

The internet is not some dark and distant place, that looks like our world but isn't. It is our world. Same world.
If I do go outside, the internet finds me.
People give me The Look, or turn away. I'll get a WhatsApp going 'I don't think they should be saying this about you at all – LINK'.
Shit just finds me. (No wonder I was the face of it.)

I guest on a live podcast. My husband overhears lads in the mens' saying I haven't got abuse at all. That it's just words. That I should toughen up.
And even now, some of you think I'm exaggerating. That it was just words and I should toughen up.
Tough? I learned from the wrath-master!
IS THAT ALL YOU LOSERS HAVE GOT? NOT ONE OF YOU'S SHOT A MYTHICAL CREATURE AND BARELY HALF OF YOU HAVE EVEN SUGGESTED I'M POSSESSED!
Maybe unless this happens to you, you can't know what it's like. To not just have a target on your back, but to be the target, a target with mad hair, going around.
I don't get anything near what women of colour get, or trans women. But this was not nothing.

Pings.

If I defend myself, I'm amplifying. I must say nothing.
If I say nothing, I'm surrendering.
It's a sheer, incessant avalanche of shit.

I get a letter from the National Library – did I forget a
return . . .? – no, they tell me they're archiving my Twitter
feed.
So, apparently you can look up nine years of jokes, and then
a sheer incessant avalanche of shit, on microfiche.

Someone doorsteps my mother. I think I spot my 'superfan'
in a shop, a lad who tweets me every day, and says he has a
knife? Does he know where we live?
A lady in an expensive trenchcoat bodyslams me in
Ballsbridge. She keeps going. Ow.

It's never 'just online'. I'm offline. You're offline. A human
being on both ends. Though I'm feeling less like one by the
day.

Coming outside was a bad move. It's floory time for Flynn.

Tara   I'm hearing my dad's voice a lot.

'Pull yourself together. Comb that hair.'

Can't.

When we were very small, Dad took us to Clare to see
Biddy's house. Seems it wasn't difficult women per se he'd a
problem with, just me.

Biddy's house is on a small hill, outside the village. A lonely
road: you wouldn't know it if you didn't know. No queues
outside it, now. Just me, my dad and sister. The cottage had
just been done up; some people were against it . . .

Seanchaí   *Touch anything belonging to Biddy and she won't be
long using her powers on you!*
*A priest gave out to Biddy one time and she stuck his horse to the
road . . .*

But do right by her and . . .
Biddy cured a neighbour's son, and saved him . . .

Dad had a fair few knocks early in life, so he feared nothing.
But he spoke Biddy's name with respect. She was a kind of
hero to him. He loved to talk about her and I was mad to hear:

Was she a witch?
(*As Dad.*) *No, a 'bean feasa'. She worked with herbs. Men in charge*
didn't like her. But she was not a witch, he said.
(Side note: nothing wrong with witches!)

The magic of it all! Dad had known old people who'd known
Biddy. Me and this past, practically touching!
I loved Biddy. The boldness of her. She'd a slatter of
husbands – fair play Biddy! But she always kept her
mother's maiden name.

Tara 'Do you want to be buried with my people?' An old
Irish chat up line.

I met my husband in London. At a bar. Yeah, we're that
couple!
He was on a date. (Told you I was possessed.) It wasn't going
well; they were on a different vibe. The barman introduced
us.
'Cute,' I thought. 'Make sure you give him the wrong
number.' I didn't though.
A fight broke out in the bar, we all grabbed our jackets and
scattered our separate ways across the city. I talked myself
out of him.
Too handsome. Too charming. American. Not for the likes of one
possessed. Anyway, I'll never see him again. London's huge. And no
way would he call.
A week later, he called.
Haunted.

'Do you want to be buried with my people?'

It was hard to describe Ireland to my American. So I brought him here, to live. I wonder, if we'd had a magic bottle, seen the future, if he'd have come . . .

Because my father's *from a different time*, it's hard to predict if he'll say something racist or not. By the time they meet, Dad has dementia. Let's just say I'm tense. In the end, he eyes my fella . . .

'Do you do judo?'

Something something foreign, something-not-hurling? It's not the worst. We'll take it. Welcome to Ireland.

Tara   I GET MY LIFE BACK.

That's what I'd scratched in my diary for the week after the referendum.

My plan: a day or two off: sleep, eat salad, back to work!! Sleep . . .

YEAH!

Insomnia. A short word for the longest nights of your life. Close my eyes? Far too scary in there . . . Every shadow an enemy, every noise a threat.

And the pings don't stop. I take a break from social media to try to cool things down, but everyone's still banging away on their hot takes.

Commenters   *'It's cosplay for her. She's no activist.'*

Tara   Never wanted to be.

Commenters   *'She just wants the fame.'*

Tara   Cos showbiz loves a mouthy dame.

Commenters   *Cosseted. Cosseted. No idea what real women go through.*

Tara   Sweetie, I don't have a job, let alone a comms team, or a driver.

Commenters   *Well, I never heard of her. She's nothing. No one.*

Tara   My input isn't required. I must STFU in this ongoing chat about me.

My agent calls: crying. Woah. I didn't know they did that. The constant swirling discussion is now the thing that's putting clients off. There's nothing we can do. I may never work again, particularly at the family-friendly end. Maybe even my chocolate boner days are behind me? Do they take rabbits on *Only Fans*? Their feet are cute . . .
The phone stops ringing. Except for tabloids, looking for *My Twitter Hell*. The story now *is* the PINGS. It's gotten fierce meta around here.

I'm visibly invisible. A freaking magician. One no one will book for children's parties . . .

The third time that my father cheated death, I was living in London. The hospital says the end is close. I fly to Cork with the funeral clothes in the bag.
He's in one of those wards with twenty-four-hour monitoring. Sleeping, mostly. Dying. They say he's dying.
And I know I'll have to tell him that I love him. Even though he once shot Santa, and knows that I'm possessed.
It's now or never, though the dementia means it's not clear he'll hear or understand.
– He once forgot that I existed, didn't know my name. You'd think you'd remember a demon child. What's a girl got to do to stand out around here? –
So, look, I don't know what good saying I love him will do, but it has to be done.

Tubes snake around. Things beep.

I dredge the words up from somewhere. They catch in my throat.
He's not strong or scary anymore. And that makes me so sad.
Closure's the thing, though there's still so much to say.
I love you, Dad.

I whisper. Like a spell.
My face gets hot. My hands in fists.
I say it.
Fists unclench. Peace made.

AND THEN HE DIDN'T.
FECKING.
DIE.

———————————————

Maybe people think I've died. If I did, would they even notice?

Seanchaí   *Bit by bit, successfully, you vanish. Like dandelion seeds, you blow away.*

Tara   My superfan now thinks I'm in the CIA and honestly, I wonder if they're hiring? I could use the work. Every day drags others in to his crusade, he whips things up. A lawyer friend tells me there's actionable defamation – I should sue.

But I'm so tired. I just want it all to stop. I just want to blow away.

PING PING PING PING PING.

Seanchaí   *You've no powers to see the future. Maybe this won't end? Would your death maybe satisfy them?*

Tara   Help me.
The doctor throws a prescription at me as I wobble into the surgery; things must look bad. The pills help with the shaking, slow my racing heart. Now. I wait.

'Trauma' is a big, dramatic word.
Living it? Mundane.
Sour milk not replaced. Bills unopened, taunting, from the hall. 'Pay me! 'Pay me!'

Go away.

Your bed, Mount Everest: you've no idea how you'll get up there, and once you're up, it's way too scary to come down.

If I could just . . . reach . . . the deodorant . . .
I'll stay here, smelly, on the floor. My breath not quite
reaching my lungs.

PING PING PING.

The rush of thoughts becomes no thought at all.

PING PING PING.

Stop it. Stop.

PING.

I think I'm going to fall. I'm falling.

And. I. Fall.

———————————

[*Ambient noise, like a party next door, or as heard underwater.*]

Tara I didn't realise that there was somewhere lower than
the floor . . . the kinda place you might not make it back
from . . .

[*Calls.*] Can anybody hear me? Am I here?

Am I underwater? Underground?

Is it nice here, or awful? I can't tell.
Remember: try to breathe. Out, then in.
What'd happen if I just forgot? Would the breathing . . .
stop? And would I . . . stop?

[*In a mirror.*] My reflection. Looks like me, but isn't. No light
behind the eyes.

I'm nothing. I'm no one.

[*Calls.*] Are you all having fun up there? Walking around,
being . . . normal?

I can't feel anything. I'm numb. Oh Jesus, am I dead
already? Have I died?

Help.

I can hear you all, up there, twisting things. What're you saying about me now? Fuck.

How in hell are emails finding me down here, I thought one of the upsides of being 'away with the fairies' was no internet.

[*Reads:*]
Can you MC this? There's no budget, but can you?
Will you publicise that? Not too much, it's not about you.
You didn't share my petition and you haven't even started ending homelessness yet.

I'm not a politician. I'm not even sure I'm a real girl anymore.
'Who does she think she is?'
'Who do *you* think *I am*?'

They're tearing at me, ripping at my flesh. Even my voice has started to go.

And even though I've vanished – banished – it's never, ever, ever going to end.

Seanchaí   *Maybe up there's not the world for you, or not your time?*
You've found the portals in between.
You could just stay here, slipped away . . .

Tara   I want to be back in my own body. Back in my flat, with my husband and the dog and the cat and the *Real Housewives*.

I've been in fight mode so long, doing nothing feels so bad. But all that's left is to go through the middle of the grief. Of what the last few years have cost, of what I've lost. It hurts. Going through the middle of it hurts.

Maybe. No.
Wait, maybe. I can do one small thing.
Say NO.

I no longer have to bite my tongue, or hold my fire.
I say NO.
Turn down email requests. Delete most social media. My
Instagram now basically my cat.
It comes out hoarse, but I say NO.

Commenters [*distant*]   *Don't let yourself be bullied off.*
Hold your ground. You're letting women down!

Tara   No. I don't work for you. I'm not your hobby and
being the focus for every single thing that's pissing you off is
way above my paygrade.
Show's over. Sorry.
NO.

[*Ambient noise stops.*]

Maybe it's time all of you watched some TV.

I find . . . a marble! Just one small, metaphorical marble.
I take one step towards the light and air.

Tara   The best thing about climbing back up to the floor, is
that everything stops.
There's nowhere left to fall. You've already been lower-than-
low.
Floor.

It's firm beneath my back. My shoulders can relax.
But it's so quiet.
I've prayed for calm. But there's no peace in this. I'm ready
for things to be normal but starting again is going to take a
full reboot. I wish I could hurry it up.

Long ago, people wore black armbands after a loss. When
you weren't quite yourself.
'Back off me, world, a bit, cos I'm not able.'
I'd like a sign, like that. But I don't have one.
I'll stay down a while longer.

We don't see anyone. My husband stops doing things, too.
I'm finding different ways of saying No.
'I'm not free.'
'I'm afraid we have an engagement.' (It's the floor.)
Or
'Arrah, I will in me hole!'

Might never sing again. Singing would require a voice, and a
kind of joy somewhere in my ribs I can't even imagine right
now. Dad would be relieved. 'Crow.'

My poor husband.
He's got the worst of me. The shell.
'Am I back yet?' I say. And he says, 'About 50 per cent.'
A half-wife.

Tara   Time slowly starts to pick up speed again.
Good things happen. Some people can still see me.
Friends offer us a holiday. Sun!
They turn up with care packages. Bubble bath and tea.
(Must not mix these up.) They worked the campaign too.
Tired and hurting. You wouldn't know their names. You
won't see them in documentaries. Amnesty gives some of us
an award, we're mentioned in another. Someone sees us.
We're grateful.

I find another marble! I'm excited! Am I better?
'51 per cent,' my fella says, 'Up from last week.'
But then a friend offers to pay for hospital time. I mustn't be
as better as I thought

All this time to think. What am I . . . for?

Would it be so terrible to stay down here forever?
Let this become my personality, my job: like women in old
novels, sent away for convalescence in the Alps, suffering
from diseases of the lung, or broken hearts. They'd whisper
my condition – 'the nerves' – like a secret, or a joke at my

expense. But I would take the air and eat cherries straight from the trees, and the joke would be on everyone else.

Sometimes, I feel something close to anger. Mid-campaign, it took a lot of energy to keep that fire in check. Dad's temper. Mine.

I flash back on a moment, asked to tell my story, live on air, while someone from the other side would be allowed to lie, for 'balance'. You know, the way they do these days, as if that's normal.
I turned it down. Said this wasn't a debate, it was my life.
That it was an insult. I might cry. (I really meant combust.)
'Wow,' the producer says, 'that would make such great radio!'
The fool. I'd have blown the speakers out. The studio would have been rubble.

Tara   Once Dad's dementia really set in, the fade took most of his fierceness away. But his fierceness was his 'himness': he was quick and clever, but also sometimes cruel.
Now he's in full-time care, a home away from home. Happy there, unsure of where he is. He's easier to be around. He needs us.
He talks about the olden days and Clare a lot.

I remember wishing I had a magic bottle like Biddy's. Wishing I could tell the future, or settle an argument. An upset stomach, even.

What is my superpower? What am I for?

Dad said that Biddy's bottle had never been found. When she died, a priest threw it in the lake, or the fairies took it back.

I have no gifts like that.

For all her gifts, even Biddy couldn't cheat death. Her story fading till it was just rumour in other people's mouths.

They say it's bad luck to profit from her memory.
(Good job this is theatre. We're safe.)
I want to honour her. I want to remember her right.

More and more, my father's stories blend to one, single
timeline: *now*. We're not sure if he's talking to us, or
someone long gone. It's all mixed up, though making sense
to him. Mum goes up to visit twice a day. Because of his
'complicated relationship' with the Church, we can never be
sure if he'll want communion when they bring it round the
ward or throw his unread newspaper at the priest's head.

That third time that my father cheated death, one young
man in his ward did not. Death came for him. The telly on.
Trolleys squeaking. The curtains drawn, the young man's
parents quietly weeping behind. A priest, doing his incense
thing. My father agitated. As we all whisper, he roars:
'THERE'S SOMEBODY FUCKING DYING IN HERE.'
We wanted the ground to swallow us up. But the floor was
just too solid.

Seanchaí   *When someone died in Ireland long ago, 'twas a party!
Keeners would come to your house for the wake. Women who'd do the
crying for you. You could take the day off – you'd be pure wrecked
from the grief. Now, keeners were often widows themselves, drawing
deep on their own pain, leading the mourning. They had the power
to usher the dead person's soul over to the other world.
Barefoot. Wild-haired. Banshee cries unleashed, summoned from the
air itself, ancient and primal.
No whispering then.
Well didn't the Church hate these difficult women. 'Twas they were
supposed to be the ones ushering you over to the other world – and
you'd pay them handsomely for it. Clerics and keeners often clashed,
wrestling for a body as it lay cooling on the table.*

*Biddy once had to tell a man that his wife had died and he on his
way to Biddy's for a cure. BUT Biddy told him this was GOOD
NEWS because . . . 'twasn't his wife at all! 'Twas a fairy
replacement! An imposter!*

He was to go home and strike her with three reeds Biddy pulled from the thatch.
When he got there, the wake was – as they say today – lit. Keeners. Neighbours. Poitín and snacks. Didn't the man strike the imposter with the sticks, and it hopped up screeching from the bed, ALIVE, and out the back door, just as his real wife waltzed back in through the front. And I'm sure there were choice words – wouldn't you be raging if your husband mistook some fairy wan for you, for ages? – leaving your beloved wandering in a dark and distant place. But all told, 'tis a happy ending.

Tara   True Crime. *Real Housewives*. Repeat.
True Crime. *Real Housewives*. Repeat.

I'm starting to take back my solid, human form. To
remember emotions, like dreams: anger, the hot one,
rumbling through me like thunder.
Joy, the yellow one, surging like sun.
Pins and needles, taking over from the numb.

I find another marble. I'm said to be at 65 per cent!

This too shall pass, and all.

Seanchaí   *On her deathbed, Biddy found a priest who'd give her last rites, and while he was praying didn't a crow outside fall out of a tree. Stone dead. Biddy brought it back to life. But she didn't save herself.*

Tara   The time comes when Dad's time's about to come. For
real. Every time the door creaks, he says his mother's name.

I don't believe in ghosts. I wish I did. He's so convinced, I
turn – he *sees* her – and it's bringing him peace.

My sister and I travel down whenever we can. Witness these
old/new conversations. Sometimes there's some pretty good
goss. Secrets slip.

We're not the family he was meant to have, you know. He was meant to have a better one.

I knew it! All along, we were just poor substitutes – me anyway. A changeling: the perfect me walking around some other place.
I bet she can wear white without spilling.
I bet she plays the harp.
I bet her hair is shiny, straight and smooth.

Three years later, on the floor, I may be too sad to wash my hair, but still I know how lucky I am. Some people live in pain forever. I know what's triggered mine.
Grief. Abuse. Public shame. They'd shove anyone off a rocker.
But, you know, I didn't die.
I've a family that loves me, a man who seems OK with living with a husk, a roof over my head. Pets! Enough to eat. (Not pets.)
So lucky –
Lads, I didn't die.
I'm putting time between me and the horrible things.

I wake one day, feeling I can chance the shop again, then break down, inconsolable, in the beans aisle. But I'm standing up. I made it to the beans!

I'm haunted.

More like my father than I thought. Maybe this is my power? To still be here. If all this had happened to someone else, they might not be. Not everyone's so lucky.
I DIDN'T FECKING DIE!!!

Tara   In all good True Crime shows, there's a trial at the end.
Not like 'trial by social media' where politicians cry about being held accountable for actually doing something actually shitty, involving our money or rights.
(Some people try to pull a fast one using *#bekind*, so *#becareful*.)

Biddy was put on actual trial, in an actual courthouse.
Accused of being an actual witch.
In the end, the witnesses withdrew their statements. They'd
been coerced into giving them anyway. They wouldn't testify
against her. Biddy was good, they said.
She was acquitted.
Biddy gave people hope. That's the story the ones who knew
her would tell.

Familiar stories re-told. Us and this past, practically
touching.

The fire in me that got me into trouble is also the spark that
drove me to speak. Got me up off the floor, helped me make
it to the beans, kept me here. It's what people called 'my
courage' (though really I was shaking so much I nearly
caused a coffee-flood).
I used to hate the bits of me like Dad.
I am like him. I'm glad.

Tara   The sky comes off . . .

The last time Dad is dying, there's one really sunny day. A
new sign hangs on his door, a symbol for anyone passing:
THERE'S SOMEBODY FUCKING DYING IN HERE.
People tiptoe, as if we might shatter.
It's quiet. Undramatic. Small.

Then, out of the blue . . .
Things get extreme.

You weren't expecting an action sequence so late in the day.
Well, neither was I, but this is what happened.

Extreme unction: the ultimate in your anointing needs.
A priest barrels in to my father's room, demolishing the
peace. Let's call him 'Father Shit'. He's dripping with
incense and oils and entitlement. I scuttle to a corner to let
him get on with it.

He's all Latin and wavey of hand. He's here to absolve Dad's
sins.
'Good luck with that,' says I. 'The man shot Santa.'
It's hard to know if Dad would want absolution or not. But
he's unaware. We let it happen.
Shit asks me to pray.
'I'll respectfully observe, Father,' I say. 'I don't believe in
ghosts.'
Holy or not, they're all the one to me.
The incense swingy-thingy freezes in mid-air. I'm rumbled.
He looks at me like priests in 70s horror films look at weirdy
girls.
He's warming up, as if to a holy high-jump, pawing the
ground; chanting and twirling his lotions and potions and
oils – oh my.

Mea culpa. Mea culpa.

He wields it like a threat. He doesn't think that it's his *culpa*
at all. Shit thinks the shit is me.

He's in a faithful frenzy. Into it. He flings stuff at my father's
head: smoke, insinuations. Spells.

I'm thinking about living a whole life – defiant, strong,
maybe even, sometimes, cruel – then lying there while other
people make your decisions. A whole big life and forgetting
it all. Are the Shits of the world so *certain* there's a god?

Breaking into these thoughts as if through a cartoon wall: it's
Shit.

He grabs my darkling hand. Too shocked to pull it back, I
stiffen. He's undeterred. He's dealt with girls like me before.
I'm powerless. Or so he thinks. He doesn't realise. I might
combust.
By my wrist, he drags me across the room. At least, I let him.
He looks like if you blew on him he'd turn to dust. He dips
my rigid fingers in the holy oil and stabs a cross on my
father's forehead with them.

I am seething. A hot tsunami in my veins. He's sucking
respect from me like a vampire – when he has none for me.

(*To herself.*) *Must not combust. Must not combust. It's a very small
town.*

I free my hand – *slip*! – and rush out to the Day Room,
where – days later – Dad will be laid out. I punch a cushion,
leave a trace in oil. My breathing starts to calm.
People will stand around here, soon, sandwiches, tea.
Looking at Dad. Telling stories about him, maybe half of
them true. He'd hate it. He'd be livid if they didn't. Soon.
It's coming soon.

When my dad died, I couldn't tell the time.
Signing in at reception, I looked from my watch to the
wall-clock, but neither of them made sense. Something . . .
wrong. Just numbers. Jumbled. Pointless.

I walked upstairs, to the room with the sign. Mum says 'He's
gone.'

She's wrong. The didn't-fecking-die guy? Dead? My father's dead?

And that is how I know there are no ghosts. Because he's
gone. He is gone-gone.

The morning of the funeral, I comb my hair for twenty
minutes. Worse. But if I don't make the effort, Dad might
just rise from the dead to say I look a fright, one last time.

At the crematorium, my husband helps shoulder the coffin.
We remember Dad in words.
We'd been told we could have two songs. After the first,
we're asked – respectfully – to *GTFO. Another family waiting.
Don't be making a meal of it. Respectfully.*
Dad ends up going two minutes early. He'd have been
thrilled – at least two punctures' worth.

Weeks later we take him up to Clare, exactly as he wished,
and lay his ashes on his mother's grave. Guess what? Biddy's
in this graveyard too, somewhere. At least, that's the story:

her grave was never marked.
But I know where Dad is. He's gone.

I can walk the shortcut along the graveyard wall like he
taught me, and find exactly where he is. I know the view
down the hill, the dip towards the village. But – to me –
they're gone.
Biddy – gone. Dad – gone. Nothing but the wind.

Seanchaí   *Your father, now, might tell it a different way?*

Tara   Every storyteller would. This is just one story. Mine.
Now, I'd love to offer you some cliché to sum everything up,
make us all feel better.
Like 'The sun always comes out'. It does. But sometimes not
enough to warm your bones. Sometimes, it's blinding.
I'm back up off the floor. Not all my marbles accounted for.
But I'm told I'm up to 69 per cent. Nice.
And my old friend the floor is there in case I ever fall again.

What we campaigned for? There still isn't abortion access for
everyone who needs it. Backslapping politicians, right back
on their knees. The world over. The past repeating. Familiar.
Re-told.

I don't comment often now. I'm not asked to. Maybe people
are worried about 'my nerves'? Or they got sick of me?
It's not my story anymore. I go to protests, but I'm happier
at the back.
We need people to tell their stories. To destigmatise, to
humanise, to tell shame where to go. Those stories and the
people who tell them might even become useful tools, that
lead to wins. Like posters! But we're not posters.
Would we do it again? I think so. We did it because we
couldn't not.
But making the private public changes things.

Tara   A year passes, from the floor, the storm. The stench around me starts – just starts – to fade. The phone rings again. Doesn't even give me a jump-scare.

I'm booked to do a festival in Clare. Of course, I visit Dad. His name on a headstone still an impossible thing. I listen, just in case. Nothing but the wind. I grab stray leaves off the gravel and go, headed for the coast.

I wonder again where Biddy's grave might be? Imagine living the life she did and having nowhere to leave flowers, or pay respects. Driving out of the village, I take a notion. Surely I can remember where her cottage was? Completely derelict now, I hear. Swallowed up by weeds. But the house is on this road. Pretty sure it's on this isolated road. You wouldn't know if you didn't know. It's been so long since I was here, with him.
Maps. Let's see if Biddy has a pin.
I pull over on the narrow strip – not a car in sight, bog on either side. I take out my phone.
No coverage.
Sure, what did I expect? So isolated. Disappointed, I note the layby, small brambly hill to the side. Still no bars. Try with the phone over my head? That's science, right? Nope. Nothing. Crap. I'd have liked to remember her right.

I drive. When I reach the nice hotel with the good wifi, I search again. Key in her name. *Where was Biddy Early's cottage?*
The map searches, pulses, pulls me in. Biddy's house was right beside that layby. Where I parked up today. It's on the brambly hill. Exactly where I stopped. Exactly.

A weak but golden sun streams in the window. Warm feeling in my chest. A tune comes to me. And, crow or not, I sing.

[*A Carpenters backing track plays,* **Tara** *sings.*]

If These Wigs Could Talk

I am a drag queen. Some of you probably already suspected that, but I wanted to be clear from the start. I became a drag queen by accident, rather than by design. Basically I slipped on a careless sequin and fell face first into MAC counter and a Whitney mega-mix. Today, queer kids decide to *become* drag queens. They see drag queens on television being famous and making lots of money, and they decide 'I want to be that too'. This is a brand new phenomenon, because drag has changed, changed dramatically. It's almost unrecognisable from the drag I fell into. So much so that I'm not sure where or how I fit in the new drag landscape.

I don't know what this new drag audience even wants from me – if it wants me at all.

Do you know what they sometimes want from me? They want me to do a gig in a GAA hall and throw myself around lip-syncing to Dua Lipa. I'm a fifty-three-year-old queen with a varicose vein who likes Dolly Parton and a comfortable seat, and the most exciting thing that happened to me last year was getting an MRI for a bulging disc. Don't ask me to do a death drop because I might have to take that literally.

Before this, generations of drag queens just fell into drag. We went to a gay bar, minding our own gay business and after a few too many Camparis we stumbled into gender discombobulation. It was stupid and fun, and a stupid fun way to put off getting a real job. At twenty-one the job is, quite literally, to get drunk for free and make a show of yourself. To be the life and soul of the party. I mean what twenty-one-year-old doesn't want that job? People often ask me 'Why did you become a drag queen?' and I always think, 'Why the fuck did you *not?!*'

But most queens eventually fell out of it again. It's a precarious way to make a living. Expensive, poorly paid, unreliable, and eventually even drag queens need to eat and pay rent and all that other boring straight stuff so they get a 'real job' – waiting tables or scamming people on Grindr or whatever – except for a small few of us who continuously kept tripping over the fun and falling forward into even more drag till one day you wake up and you're middle-aged and realise – 'I guess this is my real job'. Drag was a career for people who lived in the moment because they couldn't even picture a future.

Now my drag career trajectory has not been typical. I'd go so far as to say it's been startlingly a-typical. But it has been an absolute master class in recklessness! It started as a rebellious stunt in art college, stumbled into a nightclub, ricocheted off a mirror ball and landed in Tokyo, where I tripped and tumbled through more nightclubs and sticky stages before landing back in Dublin and falling over again and again through the dens of iniquity of a rapidly changing Ireland. And every time an opportunity for recklessness and unintended consequences presented itself, I'd look at it and think 'What's the worst that could happen?' But still, somehow, I managed to pay the rent – and have fun and promote parties and open a bar and write a book, stumble into political scandals and write shows and travel the world, and travel the world *again* with the *Irish Department of Foreign Affairs*, and become a *National Fucking Treasure*, and get honorary doctorates from august universities like Trinity where it was given to me by former President Mary Robinson – in Greek! – and did I mention that this is all the while *still in fucking drag* and with a stupid name like *Panti Bliss?!*

I mean, I cannot stress this enough: *I am not the kind of person the UN should be asking to speak in South Africa or Geneva!* I am the kind of person who does stupid things like take a fake boyfriend to Vienna to meet the Irish Ambassador.

. . .

A few years ago I'd been dating a Brazilian guy for about a year – a pretty volatile year because you know that Brazilian passion! They love a bit of drama, and Lord knows I'm always here for the drama! But we were still going strong.

He'd come to Ireland to study English and was always broke. He'd had a succession of crappy jobs – kitchen porter, stacking shelves – most of which he'd quit because they didn't give him enough opportunity to speak English.

So it's November and I get an e-mail from the Irish Ambassador in Vienna, inviting me to come to Vienna for a screening of *The Queen of Ireland* (a documentary that is ostensibly about me, but is really about Ireland) followed by a panel discussion. And they kinda sell it to me telling me how lovely Vienna is in December with all the picturesque Christmas markets, and the mulled wine, and although I'm not a Christmas markets kinda gal, I say, 'OK, sure'.

But, this fella that I'm dating – Anderson – he's very stressed. He just quit another job, he's frustrated with his English, he's missing his mammy . . . and I think, 'You know, I may not be a Christmas markets kinda gal, but you know who'd probably love Christmas markets and mulled wine in front of picturesque, snow-dusted, castles . . .?' A Brazilian who's new to Europe, has never even seen snow, and is missing his Mammy! I mean if I was Brazilian I'd think it was fucking magical!

So I got back on to the embassy and I said, 'You know, I'm thinking I might make a weekend of it with my boyfriend – go over on the Friday maybe, and of course I'll pay for the extra flight and hotel nights, I'll reimburse you if you can adjust the booking?' And they're like, 'Absolutely no problem! What a wonderful idea, we'll get that sorted.'

But I was also aware that he was a proud stubborn fucker. Like, he would never allow me to pay for *anything* – we could never go to a nice restaurant because he was stacking shelves and paying for English school and sharing a room with three others. So I thought, well . . . I could lie.

So I pick my moment, make him a Caipirinha, and then very casually say, 'You know the Irish embassy in Vienna are bringing me over for the weekend and they are more than happy to add an extra flight and extend the hotel stay.' And he's from Brazil where they have corruption down to a fine art, so he fully believes that and says, 'OK, great, tell me more about these Christmas markets you speak so highly of . . .'

Great. So I get back on to the embassy to give them his passport details, all of that, and there are e-mails back and forth, 'Looking forward to meeting both you and Anderson', 'Anderson will so enjoy the delightful Viennese Christmas markets', 'Oh! And seeing as you'll be in Vienna for the whole weekend now, the Ambassador and his lovely wife would love to invite you and Anderson to their residence for drinks to personally welcome you to Vienna, and invite you and Anderson to join them for dinner in a fancy restaurant'.

OK, lovely. That's what we're doing. Me and Anderson. We're doing that.

And then a few days before we're meant to be leaving on this delightful Viennese adventure that Anderson thinks is all a free jolly when actually I'm paying for it, he gets an interview for a job in a small restaurant, and the next day as he's leaving for the interview I say, 'Good luck! Oh! And if you get the job, remember to say to them that you can't work this weekend cos we're off to Vienna'.

He got the job! Wonderful, he's delighted, I'm delighted . . . 'And you told them you can't work this weekend?' and . . . no. He hadn't.

A *massive* row ensues. Now, I'm stubborn, but he's the world's most stubborn man, pathologically stubborn, and if you react to something with 'what the fuck?!' he will entrench and dig his heels in.

And of course I knew that – but I didn't *live* that.

It's the biggest row we've ever had. And of course during the row while we're screaming at each – 'Just call them up and tell them that you already have a fucking trip to fucking

Vienna booked this weekend, it's perfectly normal they'll be fine about it!' – I really want to scream at him: 'AND I FUCKING PAID FOR THE WHOLE FUCKING THING!' but I couldn't because . . . well because I was lying about the whole fucking thing!

It was a huge relationship-ending kinda row. I never wanted to see that stubborn unreasonable never-seen-snow-before bastard again! He could get out and never darken my perfect ass again!

He slams the door on his way out and suddenly I'm sitting there furious and staring down the barrel of a long weekend alone in fucking Vienna with nothing but Christmas fucking markets and my own seething rage. And I mean if you've ever been to Vienna you'll know it's not exactly huge craic. Lovely social housing. But not huge craic.

What the fuck was I going to do now?

So I call all my usual suspect friends. But everyone has plans and now I'm getting increasingly desperate.

And on top of everything, I'm also mortified at the idea of turning up in Vienna without my boyfriend Anderson who they are so looking forward to meeting. So even if one of my usual suspect friends was able to come it'd still be kinda mortifying to turn up with some boring Irish guy who wasn't my Brazilian boyfriend at all because I was now a single *loser*.

So really, I thought, what I really need is another Brazilian. Yeah, I need a Brazilian.

So I quickly ran through a list of possible Brazilians in my head – and quickly discounted each of them for various reasons. A Brazilian . . . Where would you find a fake Brazilian boyfriend to take to Vienna . . . tomorrow?

Grindr!

So I download Grindr (again!) and I scroll through my old chats and and I see this cute fella I'd had a fun flirty conversation with eighteen months previously. Fun enough that I remembered it and I remembered him as funny and smart. And real cute.

But this was an insane idea, right? And a long shot! He might be in a relationship, or rarely check messages. He might have moved country, gone blind, transitioned . . . he might have died! And even if none of those things were true, there was certainly a strong possibility he'd think I was a lunatic. I mean, the whole idea was ridiculous.

But, as Linda Martin has no doubt said many times: 'Desperate times call for desperate measures!'

So I messaged him.

Heyyyyy . . .

And he responds straight away!

And I say, 'Look . . . eh . . . *scrolling back through the chat* . . . Rodrigo . . . eh . . . here's the deal. Free trip to Vienna, this weekend, Christmas markets, mulled wine, trinkets, magical! Also dinner with the Ambassador and then watching a movie about, well, about . . . me . . . and also . . . pretend to be my boyfriend.

And there's a fairly long pause before he replies, 'Well, I'd have to ask my manager if I could take Monday off'.

Turns out he's a civil engineer and works as a quantity surveyor for Fingal County Council or something – who knew?! *Not me, I don't even know the guy!* And he comes back and says, 'OK she said I can take Monday off!'

Now immediately I like his manager, and I like him! Because that is very fun of him – to agree to this insane plan. Clearly Rodrigo has a reckless streak. And I am very drawn to that.

So it's agreed! Now there are still a few small hurdles to overcome like the flight – but I go online and pay €50 to change the name and passport details on the ticket. Easy-peasy. The larger issue that's going to arise however is when we actually get to Vienna and go to meet the Ambassador and his lovely wife and his name is Rodrigo and not Anderson. Hmhmmmm.

I will think on that.

So the first time I ever actually meet Rodrigo is a day later at 5:30 in the morning when I'm picking him up in a taxi on the way to the airport. And he's adorable! Handsome, smiley, and apparently totally unfazed by this insane scheme. On the flight we have two hours to learn as much as we can about each other. Because, like, what if the Ambassador's wife asks me if Rodrigo is a vegetarian while he's at the toilet in the fancy restaurant . . . well, I'd better fucking know! So we tell each other everything – siblings, hometowns, birthdays, previous jobs, favourite movies . . . and invent a backstory! When we met, how we met (we were introduced by a mutual friend at a party and now we send that friend a Valentine card every year because we're that kind of couple!). And we totally get into it like we're international spies and as we touch down in Vienna we are crying laughing at how ridiculous we are.

And we have a really fun weekend! We enjoy the many Christmas markets that the city has to offer. We take romantic pictures of ourselves rosy cheeked and wrapped up under the twinkling lights, eating piping hot bowls of goulash! We take selfies eating *Sachertorte*! I mean we're a gay rom-com come to life!

And then it's Sunday and we have to go meet the Ambassador and his lovely wife.

Now I had been thinking about how we were going to get over the name hurdle. The most obvious solution was for us to just say nothing and have Rodrigo answer to Anderson all night. But this seemed like a risky and stressful option. We'd both have to be constantly remembering to get it right, every introduction and every conversation. There would be too many opportunities to fuck up! So I had come up with a better more cunning plan.

And so we arrive at the Ambassador's residence, a rather swanky old apartment building where the Papal Nuncio lives next door, and the Ambassador and his lovely wife greet us very warmly and introduce themselves and the Ambassador's wife says, 'And this must be Anderson!' and I immediately jump in. You see, a lot of Brazilians have double-barrelled names and so I say, 'Well, it's actually, Anderson-Rodrigo, but everyone just calls him Rodrigo. Rodrigo! Or just Roddy! Isn't that right, Rod?'

And it works like a charm. Not an ambassadorial eyelash is batted and my boyfriend's name is now Rodrigo and why wouldn't it be?! *Because why on earth would we be lying about that?!*

And we have a lovely time! They're gracious hosts, we have gin and tonics, and gossip about the Papal Nuncio next door. And the Ambassador and Rodrigo get on like a house on fire! Turns out they both have engineering backgrounds so they talk maths or whatever.

So far everything was going swimmingly! We were just two couples enjoying each other's company! Well, one couple and two liars.

Then it's time for the screening so we set off for the cinema. Now I don't sit through the movie cos I've seen it, so while the movie is on we go wander romantically through one last Christmas market (really, there are a LOT of Christmas markets!) and then amble back to the theatre in time for the panel discussion which is hosted by a local radio personality, and when doing the intro to the Q&A he references my partner who is here in the auditorium and Rodrigo has to do the little half stand and wave . . . and when we're all done, the Ambassador's driver arrives to take us in his fancy car to the fancy restaurant. And it's fancy! Looks like a ship built out into the river. Rodrigo is very much enjoying the diplomatic lifestyle.

The wine and conversation flows, and at one point I'm chatting across the table to the Ambassador, and Rodrigo is chatting across the table to the Ambassador's lovely wife, and I hear the Ambassador's lovely wife say to Rodrigo something about *The Queen of Ireland* – the movie they just watched and we didn't and which is about . . . *me* . . . Rodrigo's life partner. And I hear Rodrigo reply,

'Oh, I've never seen it'.

And I think 'OH FUCK!'

And then Rodrigo says, 'You know, I just sorta feel that the movie is the public Panti, and my relationship is with the private Panti, and somehow I just feel like, for me, watching the movie would be kinda like reading his diaries or something'.

And I turn around and look at him and think 'You fucking *should* be my boyfriend!'

After dinner, Rodrigo and I walk back to our hotel a little drunk and giddy, high on successfully pulling off our ridiculous caper! We even had a little kiss.

And for a moment I could imagine bringing my fake boyfriend to meet my parents. 'He's an engineer!'. They'd have liked that. They always wanted an engineer.

. . .

When I told my parents I was gay I never really thought that they would disown me or anything like that. That's not who they are. I never doubted for a moment that they loved me and always would. But of course I worried how they'd react. You can't help it. They are from a different generation, a different time. A different *world*. They were born before the internet, before CDs, before cassettes! Before Kylie, before Madonna, before the Berlin Wall . . . went *up!* They're from *before television*. Not before *colour* television – before *television*. They were good Irish Catholics. They said the Angelus, and knelt by their bed every night to say their prayers. They had friends called Malachi and Ignatious and Concepta. They wrote *actual* letters and used abbreviations like BVM and TG (Blessed Virgin Mary, and Thank God). They were in the Sweepstakes and sometimes counted money in shillings. My dad would say 'queer' when he meant 'odd' and my mother would sing songs while doing the washing up that used the word 'gay' to mean 'cheery'.

Of course I worried.

My mum was upset at first. But my dad . . . My dad had no reaction. It was neither here nor there. I may as well have told him I like watching TV. He literally has a stronger reaction every evening at 9:30 when he sees whatever inappropriate rig-out the weather lady is wearing today.

I think what he actually said was,

'Well, don't be worrying about what I think.
What's for lunch?'

I have a theory about it.

My dad was a Mayo mountain vet, and Mayo mountain vets see life up close. They put their hands inside sheep and pull out lambs in a gush of blood and goo, and sometimes the lamb has five legs or two heads! They see adorable floppy puppies and magnificent muscular bulls. They see dead horses with grotesquely distended stomachs filled with a putrid gas that escapes with a loud hiss as they puncture the skin. They see parasites thriving as they eat away at a hapless cow's eyes. They see a chicken who's best friends with a pony! They see nature up close in all its chaotic beauty and brutality. They know that life is unpredictable and disgusting and glorious and amazing and spectacular and horrifying and wonderful and messy. They know that we can invent all the categories we want but nature refuses to be categorised, refuses to be fit neatly into neat boxes.

Nature is determinedly and resolutely odd. Resolutely queer.

Though no doubt someone will destroy my theory by introducing me to a homophobic vet. But that's OK. Because vets, like nature, are queer and refuse to be categorised.

My dad is eighty-eight now and he's not quite the same man I grew up with. He's deaf. He's frail. He gets annoyed with the hearing aids because they get lost or run out of batteries or are upside down or in the wrong ears, but he admires the elegant simplicity of his walking stick. If he can find the bloody thing.

He forgets things. But he still gets annoyed at 9:30 about what the weather lady is wearing.

He has little holes in his brain. That's what the doctor says. His brain is old and it's worn thin in places. So he forgets things. Mostly little things. Mostly. Sometimes he forgets at the end of a sentence what the beginning of the sentence was about.

Sometimes the little holes in his brain get in the way of him being him. In little ways. Just sometimes.

The first time I noticed was eight years ago when he came to the launch of my memoir – one of the last times he came up to Dublin. My dad has always been a natty dresser when he's not dressed for farms. His father was a Chief Superintendent in the Guards and he has absorbed a kind of military attitude to dressing. On Sunday mornings he polishes his shoes. And he polishes them right. He showed us how to do it right too. He doesn't buy many clothes but when he does he does that right too. He believes in quality. He is a firm believer that if you need a coat, you should buy the best coat you can afford, and then look after it for a lifetime.

My dad would dress right for his kid's book launch. Anne Doyle was going to be there. He'd pack the right shoes, the right trousers, the right jacket – the right shirt and tie to go with those trousers. He would be spick and span.

After the speeches I sat beside him. He was enjoying himself. He was proud. His shoes were properly buffed, his shirt was ironed. And his trousers were held up by a tie he'd put through the belt loops and tied in a knot.

'Dad! Why are you wearing a tie as a belt?!'

And he said matter-of-factly, *'I brought the wrong belt'*.

'You brought the wrong belt? Yeah, but . . .'. I started to point out that surely any belt – even the wrong one – was better than the knotted tie currently holding up his trousers, but I stopped. I could see my dad wasn't troubled by any doubt in his reasoning. And I suppose there was a queer kind of logic to it. My dad wouldn't wear the wrong belt, like some feckin' Weather Lady.

. . .

I flatter myself in thinking I'm like my dad in some ways. I got his sanguine-ness, his laid back-ness. His moral compass. But Dad doesn't have a reckless streak and doesn't have a career in unintended consequences.

Dad wouldn't take a dildo to *Harry Potter and the Cursed Child*.

Let me explain! See, a few years ago I was working with a big international production company – heavy hitters, big wigs – movies, TV shows, theatre. The boss of the company was a 'Sir' – Sir Colin Callander – a Knight of the Realm! Knighted for his services to the entertainment industry! They were impressive people – and lovely people. And for a few years myself and my collaborator Phillip were over and back to London regularly, excited to be working with these impressive people – and they were excited to be working with us apparently!

And they were also very excited about their *big new* show which had just opened in the West End: *Harry Potter and the*

Cursed Child. Of course they were! They'd been working on it for years, it broke ticket sales records before it even opened, and when it did open it did so to great acclaim and huge success!

So anyway, we have another meeting scheduled in London, a Monday, and we'd have to go over very early that morning . . . so the lovely people in the office suggest we make a weekend of it – come over and see the show! See friends, hang out . . .

And we think that's a great idea.

Except, you see that thing about the Harry Potter show is that it's actually *two* Harry Potter shows. Like there's Part 1 and Part 2 and they're both full length West End shows, and at weekends you can see both parts on the same day. You can spend the whole day with Harry Potter. Like . . . *the whole* . . . day. And a lot of people would really like to do that. *Clearly* a lot of people do. I mean, this thing is packing them in.

But we're not a lot of people. Like, Phillip has never read a Harry Potter book nor seen even a single Harry Potter movie. Like, he wouldn't know a house elf if he Dobby'd one! Phillip thinks Hermione is a rectal cream. He thinks Voldemort is somewhere between High Barnett and Cockfosters.

But he did still want to see it! Phillip is a theatre gay to the bone. He likes going to shows! And he did want to see the Harry Potter show because he was interested in the technical aspects. You see, the Harry Potter show is renowned for its stagecraft. There's a lot of 'magic' in the show, and apparently the technical trickery of how they pull off the magic in front of a live audience is very impressive. But Phillip could probably see most of that from seeing one of the two shows, without spending the whole of his Saturday in a theatre with a thousand over-excited tweens and Scandinavian tourists. He'd rather spend *half* his London Saturday doing that and the other half having a long boozy lunch with old friends and ending up at some dodgy club with drag queens and go-go boys in cheap jockstraps. Understandably.

And the lovely woman in the production company was all, 'But the first show ends on a cliff-hanger! You won't know what happens!' but we're guessing *Harry Potter survives?* though we don't say that.

So now we are looking forward to our weekend away. Phillip's boyfriend is going to come. And I look up an old flame in London I haven't seen in ages. I suspect there might be some unfinished sexy business there and turns out my suspicions were correct! We message back and forth and, well, you know how these things developed in the year of our Lord 2016, next thing you know we are exchanging the kind of messages that could get you arrested in large parts of the world. And he asks if I still have that one particular 'toy' I used to have in that old suitcase under my bed and . . . shoot me! I did . . . but I also think 'Oh God no! I mean, I'll just be bringing a carry on and I am *not* going through security at Dublin Airport with *that* in by bag. I mean, I'm not J.K. Rowling at a Proud Boys party, but I do get recognised. And can you imagine if some bloke with blue rubber gloves pulled a big blue dildo out of my bag in front of a hen party from Mullingar.

So, no. Sorry Bbz. Disappointed in Cockfosters.

But then Phillip mentions in passing that they are bringing a check-in bag, so . . .

I pack a check-in bag. Toiletries, a few socks, underwear, a light jacket, and a large blue dildo called Girth Brooks.

And early on a Saturday morning the three of us are on the short flight to London with nothing in the overhead bins and as I gaze down at the Welsh countryside slipping beneath us, I think . . .

All this palaver about a dildo! Airport security used to be a simple casual affair. Bloody terrorists! I mean, when you think about it, they kinda won, didn't they?! Thanks to those feckers there's security everywhere! Or at least everywhere terrorists might want to make splashy headlines. Mhmmm. If I was a terrorist what would I blow up? Wimbledon or something? Or Disneyland. Or a big West End Show! Harry Potter would be a great one! I mean that would grab headlines all over the . . .'

'Phillip . . .? Do you think they'll have security and a bag check at *Harry Potter and the Cursed Child* at the famous Palace Theatre in London's glittering West End?'

And Phillip thinks they definitely will.

Fuck.

So I come clean to Phillip and his fella Adam and explain the less than ideal situation regarding Girth Brooks in my hard-shell – and I'd like to tell you that they were surprised but they weren't.

We land in London and pick up their bag and my Chamber of Secrets and the driver is waiting for us and on the drive into the West End I figure, *I'll just brazen it out. I mean it's not like I'm doing anything illegal! I have every right to have a big blue dildo! I mean, who doesn't bring a dildo to Harry Potter . . . when they're guests of the producer who's sent a car for you and given you the best seats in the house for you and Mr Brooks?*

Oh crap!

The bag check is *literally* ON THE PAVEMENT in front of the theatre. In broad fucking daylight, in front of hundreds of excited Harry Potter fans and every passing tourist. I mean there are large tables sitting out on the fucking pavement with security people throwing bags onto them and opening them up, right there, surrounded by squealing groups of kids and hassled parents, separated from the hustle and bustle of the West End by nothing more than a fucking rope. They are opening bags in full view of what seems like the whole fucking world.

Fuck.

Phillip and Adam are looking at me like *arms folded*.

OK, I gotta think. Well, first things first, gotta collect the tickets. So I go into the box office at the side of the theatre, and give a friendly man my name.

'Oh yes! We have your tickets here Panti!' and hands me an envelope. And then adds 'There are VIP security passes in there too'.

VIP security passes!

I go back out, hand Phillip and Adam their tickets, and triumphally announce 'We have VIP security passes!' and smugly head back round to the front of the theatre ready to wave our passes as we sweep into the theatre with a casual dildo. We look around and see a sign – 'VIP SECURITY' . . .

And it is *literally* just another fucking table on the pavement beside the non-VIP table. Exactly the same, it just has a shorter line.

Exfuckeramous!

From the line I can see the uniformed woman working the VIP security table – a chatty middle-aged Black woman with a London accent, apparently quite enjoying her job. She's getting people to open their bags and then going through them, lifting things out, giving them a squeeze, asking occasional questions.

Then it's my turn and as she beckons me to the table, I'm not sure why, but I think to myself, 'Gay it up!' For some reason I think being flaming and flamboyant and unthreatening is the best plan of action. So I lift my case up on to the table, and say 'Heyyyyyy Gurl!'

And the security woman – let's call her Carol – Carol knows a homosexual when she sees and hears one so she says 'Heeyyyy!' and I like her immediately. Like, I'd say Carol is fun to go out with.

I can see myself and Carol putting the world to rights at 4am over a bottle of Goldschlager we found under the sink at some random gay's afterparty.

'Can you open your bag for me?' Carol asks and as I do I'm thinking on my feet, and say 'Phew! Made it. Came straight from the airport!'

I'm trying to establish a connection with Carol. I want Carol to be my friend, because friends don't embarrass friends in front of Harry Fucking Potter.

'Oh?! Where you from?'

'Dublin. I mean I've come from Dublin today. But I'm not . . . I'm from Mayo. But I flew from Dublin,' I ramble incoherently as I mentally try to map my bag and pinpoint exactly where the Philosopher's Dildo is. Carol opens my case out and I know on this side there's my wash-bag, jacket, sweater, phone battery, and on this side there's socks, underwear, t-shirts, and, wrapped in a cotton tote bag, the Dildo of Azkaban.

'Dublin?! You came over specially for the show?' she asks as she starts rummaging around and pulls out my washbag, unzips it and starts poking around.

'Yaaaas! Big Harry P fans! *Wingardium Leviosa* Gurl!' as Carol pulls a condom out of my wash bag and then immediately slips it back in with a hint of a grin.

'Oh Gurl, I'm sure you must find all sorts in these bags! Haha! Like all sorts, right? Ooh I bet you have some stories Kween!'

And she laughs as if to say yes, but it's unconvincing cos after all she's checking bags at Harry Fucking Potter not working the coat check in The Berghain!

And then she puts down my wash-bag and in what seems like slow motion, she moves her hands – past sensibly dressed tourists and people on their way to Primark, past stressed parents and squealing sugar-smeared children waving plastic fucking wands – and she places them firmly on the cotton tote bag of the dildo of Diagon Alley and gives it a gentle probing squeeze, and . . .

I lean forward, put my hands on hers, look Carol straight in the eyes with all the unthreatening intensity I can muster, and say . . .

'Please don't open that in front of the children.'

And Carol looks at me.
And I look at Carol.
And Carol looks at me.
And I look at Carol.

And for a moment, although surrounded by hundreds of squealing children and a large portion of the world's tourist trade, time and space collapse in on themselves and there is only me and Carol, suspended in this infinite moment, tethered to each other by a gossamer of consciousness, our eyes locked, as pure energy flows between us through the vacuum of space where once was England . . . and Carol lifts her hands, closes my bag in one sweeping motion, and says

'Enjoy the show.'

I fucking love Carol. I would die for Carol. I would go to Azkaban for Carol. I would burn Hogwarts to the fucking ground for Carol.

And inside the lobby of the theatre, my God the rush! The exquisite, ecstatic rush of recklessness! The rush of taking a dildo to Harry Potter on the invitation of a Knight of the Realm! And a little later as we sat in our excellent seats in the heightened dark of the theatre with the Dementors flying above our heads, I pictured the dildo snug in the cloakroom and thought, 'Girth Brooks would be really impressed with the stagecraft'.

. . .

The movie that Rodrigo has never seen, *The Queen of Ireland*, is ostensibly about me, but the real stars of the movie are my parents. Everyone who watches it falls in love with my parents.

And after the movie went out into the world something unexpected started to happen. Something that is simultaneously beautiful and lovely, but at the same time, also crushingly sad.

My mother started getting letters. Letters from London, and Berlin, and New York, and Sydney. Shout out to An Post who delivered one that was simply addressed to 'Panti's Mammy, Co Mayo, Ireland'. The letters were all from older Irish men who had left Ireland in the 60s/70s/80s – men who had run out of Ireland – driven out – by a country that didn't want them. Men who knew they could never be themselves and call Ireland home. Men who had *escaped*. Men who wanted their story to be happier and more honest than it ever could have been had they stayed, so they decided that if Ireland didn't want their stories, they would write them in Melbourne or Chicago or Singapore instead. And it was Ireland's loss. Many of these men wrote brilliant, successful, exciting stories in these other places. Stories that Ireland could have benefitted from – but didn't want to. And in the many years since, they had never told their own mothers why they had left and why they had never returned. And now, it was too late. They'd never have the opportunity to tell her now.

So instead they sat down at kitchen tables in London and San Francisco and Paris and wrote to my mother instead. As a kind of stand-in or surrogate for their own mammy. They told *my* mammy *their* stories.

And my mammy is a letter writer. She's a sender of birthday cards and best wishes and get well soon's and all the town's gossip and 'no dessert till you write your aunty that thank you note!' So she writes back. And now my mother has this odd collection of older gay penpals around the world. And it's lovely. It's beautiful. And it's also desperately, pathetically sad. Shamefully sad. This unnecessary cruelty inflicted by Ireland on its sons. My mother and her penpals, whose stories she knows and keeps to herself.

. . .

I got into drag for the same reason people go into dentistry – because I was angry. I was a nineteen year old gay boy in a country that literally criminalised my sexuality – and I'd only just found out how good I was at doing the crime! Being gay and doing the crime was all I wanted to do at the time.

I was twenty-five-years-old before it stopped being a crime. Twenty-five! People my age got mortgages when they were twenty-five. And this country treated me and my kind *like* criminals. But unlike other crimes, we weren't treated innocently until we actually committed the crime, we were *pre-punished*. Punished if they even *suspected* we wanted to do the crime. And it didn't take much to arouse suspicion – a limp wrist, a high pitched giggle, a colourful shirt, a Madonna album. And while most of us didn't end up in prison, plenty of us did end up hurt, humiliated, ostracised, embarrassed, ridiculed, disowned, and yes, dead. Often dead. Oh not so many of us beaten to death like Declan Flynn in Fairview Park, but plenty of us bullied or harassed into doing it ourselves. And while some of the punishments were petty indignities like being forced to explore your sexuality in a grotty public toilet with strange older men while everyone else got to kiss boys in rented tuxedos at the debs, others were unimaginably worse. Whole swathes of us

killed by a big disease with a little name while people
cheered or just looked away – and made those deaths even
harder to bear by heaping blame and shame and just
desserts into the rows of empty pews where family and
neighbours were meant to be but weren't because even
knowing us in death was shameful.

So yes, I was angry. I had plenty of reasons to be angry. And
worse than that, I was angry and lonely. A lethal
combination. The kind of desperate combination that leads
people to hurt themselves and others. So luckily for me I
managed to find other queer people – no easy task at a time
when queer people sensibly kept themselves hidden from a
world that despised them.

Of course, they did! We were queer in a society where you
couldn't be queer and also take part in that same society. All
the things my straight brother was supposed to aspire to
weren't even available to me. You couldn't be queer and get
a good job. You couldn't be queer and get married. You
couldn't be queer and have kids, go to church, be one of the
lads, be on telly, be a teacher, a footballer, a barrister . . . You
could hide your queerness and hope for the best. Most
queers did. Sensibly. They learnt the fine art of invisibility as
a defence mechanism. A lonely kind of superpower.

But I found them, these people like me. I found them
hidden in basements and side-streets, behind unassuming
doors and blackout curtains. I found them under mirror
balls and strobe lights. Dancing and kissing and laughing on
dance floors, making friends and families and lovers. I
found them falling in love and falling into bed with
hairdressers with frosted tips in bedsits in Rathmines and
fucking as if their lives depended on it – because they did. I
found them having fun. Living and loving defiantly, building
life rafts from music and sex and friendship.

These people like me that I found in hidden basements were
mostly radicals. Of course they were! Just being there was a
radical act! Dancing in a world that despises you is a radical

act. Having fun in a world that wishes you were dead is a radical act. And fucking in a world that criminalises fucking is *literally fucking radical*.

But we weren't radicalised in these basements though. We weren't radicalised by Donna Summer and poppers. We were radicalised before we even got there by the outside world that despised us.

And in a world that despises you, refusing to be invisible was radical and brave and defiant.

Do you know who isn't invisible?

I'll give you a clue.

Drag queens.

The first time I saw a drag queen she wasn't blending into the background! She was covered in sequins to make damn sure she didn't! She was big and bright and bold and colourful, reflecting light and *demanding* attention. She had a bloody spotlight! She was *anti*-invisible!

And she wasn't terrified her wrist would betray her! She wasn't trying to suppress any hint of terrifying femininity. She had taken all of these things that you were afraid of, all these things they tried to sneer out of you, all of these things they told you were weakness, and she was throwing them back at you as *strength*. As *power. As fun!* It was inherently punk. It was and gloriously reckless! An act of exuberant defiance. She was giving all those assholes the glittered finger and it was the most beautiful thing I'd ever seen.

Of course the world has changed since then. Being queer in the world has changed since then. Queerness isn't a crime anymore. Although Jane McDonald's cover of 'Ray of Light' is right on the line. Gay bars aren't hidden in inconspicuous basements anymore. Like mine, they're visible, conspicuous, and unashamed. And they're not filled with radicals anymore. You don't need to be radical to find a gay bar anymore.

And drag has changed since then. It's not very angry anymore. It's been packaged and polished. Commodified, televised, and advertised. De-fanged and Instagrammed.

And yet . . . And yet . . .

I'll go into a gay bar somewhere and I see some twenty-year-old kid on stage. His first time in drag, wearing a dress he borrowed off his sister, a cheap wig he got off the internet, one eye-lash already peeling off, lip-syncing badly to his favourite Ariana Grande song – and he's loving every gaudy second of it!

And maybe he's never had a political thought in his life! He wouldn't know Judith Butler from Jean Butler! But it doesn't matter. Because what he's doing is *still* a political act, still radical! He's still rejecting conformity, up-ending convention. Whether he can articulate it or not, what he's doing is still a defiant act of rebellion – against school-yard bullies, and prissy neighbours, and mouthy straight blokes in Temple Bar. What he's doing is a sequinned refusal to be cowed. He's here, he's queer, get used to it or go fuck yourself.

Somehow, despite it being mainstreamed and commercialised and polished and repackaged, drag retains this essential kernel of queer resistance and radical reckless defiance.

I look at that twenty-year-old kid and I know why he's in drag.

But I'm not twenty, so why am I still in drag? What am I for now?

. . .

I very nearly became one of my mother's penpals. When I was the same age as that kid in the drag bar I packed my drag bag and ran out of this country and didn't look back. Not once! I was glad to see the back of the place. This place that didn't want me. You don't want me? Fine! I don't want you either. And to prove it I picked a place as far away and different from here as I could imagine. Tokyo. And I didn't miss Ireland. Not for a second. Why should I? It didn't miss me. It was glad to see the back of me.

And I couldn't have picked anywhere better to forget Ireland. No one in Japan has a fucking clue where Ireland is. They have absolutely no concept of this place. When people ask where you're from and you say Ireland, they think you said Iceland. 'You must be very good at skiing!' they say. And for a while, I would correct them, try to explain. But then I realised I didn't care and it was just easier to nod and agree, yes, I'm from Iceland, I'm a great skier. And Tokyo in 1990 was a great place to be if you didn't want to meet Irish people. You could go years without meeting one or even hearing of one. People never said, 'Oh, I know another guy from Iceland'.

And that suited me. I didn't want to meet other Irish people. I didn't want to be reminded of this place that hated me. I didn't want to have to pretend to miss it – because I didn't. I didn't want to have to pretend to be dying for a Barry's tea, or wax lyrical about Tayto and 'Mayo for Sam!'

About four years into my time there I was working in a huge nightclub spread over seven floors in an industrial part of the city. An achingly cool kinda place and they paid me to run around and be the life and soul of the party. And one night, in March, I turned up at work and the manager immediately grabbed me and said 'Panti-chan! Tonight there are a group of people from Iceland coming to the club to celebrate King Patrick's birthday!' and I looked at him and said, 'Do *not* tell the people from Iceland that I am also from Iceland!' And then I ran around the club before we opened and told every staff member, 'Do *not* tell the people from Iceland that I'm from Iceland'.

Because I wasn't. I wasn't from anywhere. I renounced my Irishness in favour of drag. Drag queens weren't from Ireland. They were from wherever they wanted to be from.

And I didn't want to be from anywhere. I was Panti, from nowhere. I was just Panti.

Of course obviously I feel very different about Ireland now. Time and drag heals all wounds. I found my way back. This place doesn't scrub off so easily. It clings to you like lichen on a damp rock. I love being Irish now. I love being in Ireland. But not because I changed. I didn't. Because Ireland changed. I was still the same queen who'd been pushed out – but I came back with a better understanding of my drag superpower. I had left because I felt excluded – not just from the country, but from Irishness *itself*. The country I left had a very rigid definition of Irishness, a whole list of boxes you had to tick and I didn't tick most of them. There was no box for queerness. I had left because there was no room for me here – but Panti doesn't get squeezed out. She makes room. Look at me! It's hard to ignore this. It's hard to pretend you haven't seen me. I'm big, I'm loud, I've got a lot of hair. And all of this makes me feel powerful in the world, it amplifies my voice, and I had something I wanted to say. I had a project.

A project to expand the definition of Irishness. To make it more elastic so it would stretch around someone like me. And I wasn't the only one who wanted to do that, there were lots of us! It was a collective effort. I had a mission and my weapon of choice was drag. An outsized and un-ignorable queerness. A colourful unashamed joyous queerness that couldn't be shrunk or diminished or squeezed out. And we succeeded in that project I think. Eventually. You *can* be queer and fully Irish now. It's practically mandatory!

So what am I for now?

. . .

The last time my Dad made the trip to Dublin – the last time he was able to – we went to see a big Caravaggio exhibition in the National Gallery together.

The gallery, like the country it represents, has changed a lot since I would go there as an art student in the 80s. I spent a lot of time there back then, doing what people have always done with pictures – trying to see myself in them. I'd stand in front of them, gazing, looking for evidence of me – or at least people like me. And every now and then – it's the right day, the right picture, the right light – suddenly what you see is *you*, reflected back at you through someone else's eyes, and you feel seen by someone who made this picture maybe centuries ago.

And somehow you feel less lonely, because, when you are the weird art student kid in the grey, aggressively normal Dublin of 1986, and you've taken the 46A into town and the whole trip was tense, but also so boringly familiar because an interchangeable little gang of Saturday teenage assholes thought they were hilarious and the first people to point out that you looked like a faggoty clown – which in fairness, they weren't wrong – but when you're that kid, it feels so good to see another faggoty looking clown gazing back at you from those walls. Even if he's only a bit player – someone in the crowd cheering on racing horses, a passer-by in a marketplace, a drunk playing cards, or an apostle crowding round a ripped Jesus (or even Jesus himself!) – it feels good to know there have always been faggoty looking clowns. And some of them even got to be Jesus.

It feels good because it is – *literally* – life affirming. Queer life affirming.

It feels good because it gives you a sense of being rooted in the world. You aren't some ephemeral glitch. A biological hiccup. We're meant to be here. People like me have always been here. And there's the proof, right there, in the corner behind King Whatshisface the Third, entertaining the other drunks by doing the Dance of the Seven Veils with half eaten chicken drumsticks.

I think I saw that queen perform in the George once.

My dad had wanted to see the big Caravaggio exhibition that he'd been reading about, so I took him, and we stood quietly among the crowds who'd also come to see this flashy exhibition. We stood together in front of one lovingly painted handsome man after another, each bathed in the artist's famous light, reflecting off pale sensual skin revealed beneath soft shirts that always appeared to be slipping off their toned, defined bodies, whether they were dramatically protecting Jesus from muscular soldiers or just quietly peeling a moist fruit, until . . .

We find ourselves standing in front of a painting of a rather camp teenage boy, who is reacting . . . *theatrically* . . . to being nipped on the finger by a little gecko, and I'm thinking, 'Ooh Gurl! He even has the same big mop of curly hair that I had at that age, and can you imagine the drama if I'd been bitten by a gecko on that campsite in France when we were kids!' And my dad – who's been in quiet contemplation since we arrived twenty minutes ago – suddenly announces, very loudly – to everyone! – because his hearing aid was in upside down:

'Caravaggio . . . Definitely one of your lot! He'd be drinking in your place alright.'

I think my Dad just gay life affirmed me!

. . .

I get asked a lot about marriage equality. A *lot*! Because I somehow found myself in the somewhat uncomfortable position of being a poster girl for same sex marriage. I say 'uncomfortable' because I've never really been the marrying type. Even during the campaign, I always figured marriage wasn't for me but if gays want to get married and be as boring as everyone else, they should be able to. Who am I or anyone else to stop them? Live your best life, Gay! Get your dull suburban life, Queen! Tie that Butch Dyke down, Femme! But even after the referendum I'd say to young queers, 'Just cos you can get married doesn't mean you have to get married! Have you considered joining a lesbian commune?'

But despite my own reservations about marriage, I was never so proud of this country and of being Irish as I was the day the referendum result was announced. That this country, that once tried so hard to disown me – and nearly succeeded! – had now collectively embraced me and my kind, was overwhelming. Miraculous almost. I wanted to run round that Tokyo nightclub again and take it all back. 'I am from Iceland!! Reykjavik for Sam!'

. . .

There is a power in Ireland's recent story. Before the pandemic I would tell it often, and often in places where it can be extremely difficult, sometimes dangerous, to be queer.

Places like Bosnia-Herzegovina.

I did my show at a small theatre in Sarajevo once. Outside the theatre they had large poster sites to advertise the shows with bright attention-grabbing pictures. But not for my show. The posters for my show were basic black and white text. No pictures. The theatre was nervous about attracting too much attention. There'd never been a drag queen in Sarajevo before. Apparently.

There's no gay bar in Sarajevo either. There is a kinda misfit bar. Off the main drag. The kind of bar that might have a few gays at a couple of tables, a few punks or goths at another. Maybe a couple of fashion students at another. The kind of bar we had in Dublin when I was a student in the 80s. The bar had been attacked by neo-Nazis three times in the previous few months. The last time, the barman had been dragged outside and beaten badly.

The night of my show the theatre had organised extra security. They had also liaised with the local police just in case. During my show I told Ireland's story, and afterwards in the theatre bar I did a meet and greet with the audience and we had a few drinks together. I took a selfie on my phone with one of the extra security men – because he was hot – but afterwards in my dressing room the theatre manager came to me and asked me to delete the picture. The security man was worried I'd share it online where people could see it and there'd be repercussions for him.

In the bar a young woman approached me. She was about seventeen. A lesbian. She thanked me for coming to Sarajevo, but it was me who should have been thanking her. Coming to my show was a small act of defiance – even bravery. It's not easy to be a seventeen-year-old lesbian in Sarajevo. It can be difficult and sometimes dangerous, and at seventeen it can seem overwhelming and hopeless.

I consider myself very lucky to be able to tell a seventeen-year-old lesbian in Sarajevo Ireland's story. Our story. To tell her that when I was her age, Dublin wasn't very different to Sarajevo. To tell her that at seventeen, I too thought that things would never be different, that things couldn't possibly change so enormously.

To tell her a story that starts in hidden basements but ends in the sunshine of a castle courtyard on a referendum day. To tell her how seventeen-year-old lesbians in Dublin used to be afraid to hold hands at a bus stop too. Maybe not because they were afraid they'd be beaten on the pavement, maybe not even because some asshole would abuse them – but because they were afraid of being alone. Afraid that some asshole would say something – 'fucking dykes!' – and the rest of the people at the bus stop would quietly agree and say nothing. They were afraid of that. And how lovely it is to tell her that now, those young women are very much less afraid, because even if some asshole says something, since the referendum they know that *at least 64 per cent of the people at this bus stop think you're the asshole!*.

Ireland's story proves that deep and dramatic social change *is* possible, and it's possible in a relatively short period of time. Ireland's story is a story of possibility and hope. And to seventeen-year-old lesbian in Sarajevo, it's a lifeline.

There is a power in Ireland's story, and it's a story that is a privilege to tell.

. . .

There was no youth club in Ballinrobe when I was growing up there – and even if there was I wouldn't have felt comfortable there.

The other boys with their footballs, and me with my *Charlie's Angels* scrapbook.

And yet, not long after the referendum, I was asked to go back to Ballinrobe – at the invitation of the Ballinrobe Youth Club. They wanted me to help launch a booklet – a guide to coming out! Written, designed and produced by the youth club! And I went, and found myself giving a little speech in the afternoon, with the old lady who used to sell me comics on my way home from school – even older now – on a plastic chair in the front row beside my parents, and the local Garda in the back just having a scope. And one of the kids from the club also spoke – a tall confident sixteen-year-old with an an Eastern European name, a Mayo accent, and gold nail polish. The whole thing *blew my fucking mind*. I had to get out my phone and check with Google Maps that I really was in Ballinrobe County Mayo and not some parallel universe. But it was Ballinrobe. This really was the same place I'd grown up in.

And as the lonely awkward schoolboy I used to be, fell madly in love with this boy with gold nails who would never have to write letters to my mother, the fifty-four old drag queen I am today wondered again: so what am I for now?

I used to be so sure! But I wasn't at all sure for a while. There aren't many role models for ageing drag queens anyway. Most ageing drag queens quietly bow out and do accounting or pilates. And there are thousands and thousands of baby drags now to make you feel old – more now than I ever imagined possible! They multiply like Gremlins every time they're exposed to another season of *RuPaul's Drag Race*!

So what am I for now?

. . .

My father always knew what he was for. Outside of us I mean. Beyond family, beyond being a father and husband. He was for sick animals and worried farmers. He was for rough-hewn Mayo mountains and rough-hewn Mayo mountain men. He was for calming panicked sheep and grappling with obstreperous cattle. For striding through wet grass and pulling on wellies, and smelling of outdoors and damp and disinfectant. He was for telling people not to worry – the dog would be fine – What's for lunch? – and taking a lake trout as payment cos times were hard. My dad always knew what he was for, till time and tired bones and more and more little holes took that knowing away from him.

Maybe it was the pandemic's fault, but for a while it was taken away from me too. I really did start to wonder: *What the fuck am I for now?* I spent the best part of two years lying on the sofa eating chocolate Kimberly because all the things I'd thought I was for had been whipped away overnight. My life as it was had been turned off. No more running around clubs, no more stages, no more shows, no more speeches, no more Pantibar. All these things that I'd always thought I was for, all these things that made up who I was every day were suddenly . . . disappeared. Overnight. Without me having any say in the matter. And between my afternoon gins and the next chocolate Kimberly I had a kind of existential crisis. *'What am I even for anymore?'*

And do you know where I found the answer to that question? Or where I was *reminded* of the answer? Of all fucking places, Mayo!

Mayo was having its first ever Pride march, in Westport (which arguably isn't really in Mayo – I mean, I think of it more as a middle class enclave surrounded by Mayo) and being one of the only notable homosexuals from Mayo (and obviously the hottest one) I was invited to be Grand Marshall. And it was lovely! The weather was gorgeous, the sun shone on the adorable colourful parade as it wound its way through the picturesque, middle class, annual Tidy Towns Competition winner (if you're sensing slight hint of sarcasm, I'll just point out that nothing runs as deep as the quiet vein of resentment that the rest of Mayo feels about Westport) but it was gorgeous. Half the town in the parade and the other half standing in shop doorways or outside pubs, waving us by – till we ended up by the seashore where there was a friendly family afternoon of dancing and performances and speeches.

Now, around the time that the little party of maybe a hundred people was due to be winding up, there was a Drag Queen Story Time planned at a local bookshop just a couple hundred metres from where we were, and one of the younger drag queens was dressed in a pretty princess gown ready to skip down there and entertain a small group of little kids who were waiting eagerly with their parents.

But I could see that she was nervous. And she was right to be.

For weeks now, since the Story Time had been advertised online, the bookshop where it was going to be, had been the target of an organised online far-right hate campaign. And the increasingly abusive comments had spilled offline as the shop was targeted with endless threatening phone calls, and at the little party by the seashore we got word that a small but angry group of fascists had indeed turned up, intimidating the shop owners and the parents and small kids who'd turned up for the Story Time.

Of course the young drag queen was understandably nervous.

So I did what any older, seen-it-all-before, loud-mouth drag queen who'd been driven out of this country once before, would have done. I took the microphone and told everyone we were going to go meet some arseholes. And off we set, this colourful rag-tag bunch, along the waterfront, in the late afternoon sunshine of a Mayo summer. And let me tell you – drag is a superpower. It transforms you – a mere human – into a colourful, larger-than-life, unignorable, powerful, multi-gendered, fearless and fearsome Warrior Queen. And when the fascists saw this giant pink reincarnation of Grainne Mhaol sailing down the road towards them, trailed by a Pied-Piper Pride Parade of rainbow flags and face-painted teenagers, they visibly shrank beneath the signs they were waving – which accused us of badly spelled crimes. One large-chested woman managed to muster up the courage to un-ironically and loudly demand to know why I was parading around with breasts in front of children, before the leader of the group (a man, you'll be shocked to hear, well known as a far right agitator and with a string of convictions) started aggressively shouting at me, demanding to know if I had 'Garda clearance' to speak to the teenagers around us on the now noisy and chaotic pavement outside the bookshop.

His question was a tactic. Fascists have to invent threats posed by drag queens because the real threats posed by drag queens are actually fabulous. We threaten you with a good time. We threaten you with glitter turning up in your crevices for weeks afterwards. So instead they pretend we're monsters.

'Do you have Garda clearance to talk to these fifteen-year-olds?!' he demanded angrily, and I replied,

'I have Garda clearance to tell you to go fuck yourself.'

Unluckily for him, and luckily for Mayo Pride, this exchange was caught on twenty phones, and an hour later it was spreading across the internet and a few hours after that – showing the wily cunning that Mayo people are renowned for – Mayo Pride was raising money for an even bigger and better Pride next year by selling t-shirts and tote bags emblazoned with the slogan, 'I have Garda clearance to tell you to go fuck yourself'.

And while our heroine young queen inside the bookshop shook off her nerves and spun a magical tale for an audience of enraptured kids, I looked at those miserable fools with their miserable signs shouting on the pavement outside and realised that, in a way, I should be thanking them.

I'm old enough to remember exactly where we've come from and I refuse to go back there. And I'm too old and too long in the tooth to stand by while a baying mob tries to drag us back there.

You know Martin Luther King was wrong about one thing. The arc of the moral universe does *not* always bend towards justice. History is littered with examples of times when things went backwards and we are in one of those moments right now. All around the world, and here at home, reactionary and regressive movements have been left to fester and grow and organise till they are pushing and bending that arc backwards. And their strategy is to find weak spots and exploit them by fanning the flames of moral panics and hidden fears. And one of the weak spots they think they've identified is the queer community – and in particular the trans community. Like all bullies they've tried to single out what they perceive to be the smallest and weakest link. To separate them from the queer herd.

Fuck that! And if you aren't trans, or aren't part of the queer community and think it doesn't effect you? Oh don't worry – they'll work their way up to you. They've already started on women's reproductive rights, and immigrants, and bolstering the supremacy of whiteness, and the list is getting longer and longer. The trans community are one of the canaries in the coal mine and you're already breathing noxious fumes. And yet even as you inhale the expanding cloud of hate, comfortable men and comfortable women will line up to tell you you're overreacting, you're exaggerating, calm down, ignore the increasingly desperate chirping of the panicked canary and breathe.

On a pavement outside a book shop in County Mayo I remembered that I'm for the same thing I've always been for – to tell them to go fuck themselves.

Now is the time! Now is the time to find your superpower and fight back. Now is the time to protect what we've achieved. Now is the time to put our collective shoulder to the arc of the moral universe and bend it back towards justice.

Now is the time to use your Garda clearance and tell them to go fuck themselves because I told that girl in Sarajevo that everything would be better and I refuse to let them make a liar out of me.

. . .

After I'd had the little kiss with Rodrigo in Vienna on our way back to the hotel from the fancy restaurant, I wondered out loud: 'Maybe we should be boyfriends' and Rodrigo said 'maybe' . . . but he wasn't sure my story with Anderson was fully finished – even though it definitely was! In fact I was so sure that a few days after we got back I was doing a Christmas gig in the Project Arts Centre, and I end up telling a packed theatre about taking a fake boyfriend to Vienna, and the audience was drunk and full of Christmas cheer and by the end there are two hundred people on their feet chanting 'RODRIGO! RODRIGO!' and I suddenly felt a pang of guilt for inadvertently turning an auditorium of Saturday night drunks into a baying mob who hated my ex boyfriend Anderson.

I'm still friends with lovely Rodrigo. We still giggle about our Viennese adventure.

And that stubborn prick Anderson? Well, dear Reader . . .

I married him.

And Rodrigo came to the wedding.

. . .

'How's Anderson?'

It's always the first thing my dad asks me.

'How's Anderson?'

He has a lot of little holes in his brain but he's never forgotten Anderson's name.

'How's Anderson?' And he really wants to know. He really wants to know how Anderson is. He likes Anderson.

When we got married, my dad was delighted. Happy for me and Anderson. Proud.

You could see your face in his shoes. He wore his very best. And the right belt.